José Antonio Primo de Rivera

Anthology of Speeches and Quotes

José Antonio
Primo de Rivera

ANTHOLOGY of SPEECHES and QUOTES

ANTELOPE HILL PUBLISHING

Fourth printing, 2025.

Originally published by *Ediciones Prensa Del Movimiento Madrid* in 1950, an arm of *Cadena de Prensa del Movimiento*, or 'Press Network of the Movement,' a journalistic group and publishing house that belonged to the *Falange Española Tradicionalista y de las JONS*, the single party allowed in the Francoist state. During the transition from dictatorship to democracy, the Press Network of the Movement was renamed to the State Social Media and was continuously dismantled until its liquidation in 1984.

This work is being reprinted in English by Antelope Hill Publishing as it is an out-of-print work deemed worthy of preservation in physical form. The changes that were made were the moving of the glossary from the end to the beginning of the book and the inclusion of the Twenty-Six Point Manifesto of the Falange at the end as an appendix.

Cover art by Swifty
Edited by Taylor Young
Formatted by Margaret Bauer

Antelope Hill Publishing | antelopehillpublishing.com

Paperback ISBN-13: 978-1-956887-37-2
EPUB ISBN-13: 978-1-953730-16-9

The Falangist Oath

I swear to give myself always to the service of Spain.

I swear to have no pride other than that of the fatherland and of the Falange and to live under the Falange in obedience and joy, impetuousness and patience, gallantry and silence.

I swear fidelity and submission to our leaders, honor to the memory of our dead, and imperturbable perseverance amid all vicissitudes.

I swear, wherever I may be, in order to obey or in order to command that I shall respect our Hierarchy from the first to the last rank.

I swear to reject and give no ear to any voice of either friend or foe who might weaken the spirit of the Falange.

I swear to preserve above all the idea of unity: unity among the lands of Spain, unity among the classes of Spain, unity within the individual man and among the men of Spain.

I swear to live in holy brotherhood with all members of the Falange and to lend every assistance and eliminate every difference whenever this holy brotherhood requests that I do so.

CONTENTS

Part Three: Practical Mandates

INTRODUCTION

FROM THE ORIGINAL 1950 PUBLICATION

The compiler of this Anthology prefaced his work with an admirable introduction, which will be read with advantage by those who are acquainted with Spanish. This version, however, is intended for those who do not read that language, to most of whom José Antonio Primo de Rivera is only a name, a name at times confused with that of his father General Primo de Rivera, or even unknown altogether. The original introduction was written for the Spanish people, to whom José Antonio is a household word, and his portrait, exhibited everywhere in the country, is as familiar as that of General Franco himself.

It seemed best, accordingly, not to translate Sr. Torrente's introduction, much of which would inevitably leave the English-speaking reader at a loss, but to substitute the present sketch. In compiling it, the translator has avoided any attempt at a literary essay; still less does he seek to pass judgment on José Antonio as a historical or political figure. He has only sought to provide that framework of facts which will enable the reader to follow the course of the Anthology without getting puzzled on points of detail, and to appreciate José Antonio's doctrines more fully by an acquaintance with the environment in which they were expressed and out of which they arose. Those, therefore, who are well informed on the history of recent Spanish politics and thought are asked to excuse the repetition of facts already familiar to them but perhaps indispensable to others.

A skeleton of Spanish history over the last thirty-odd years might be constructed as follows. In the Great War of 1914–18, Spain was neutral. She had no direct interest involved. She was still weak and depressed after the loss of her last American possessions, Cuba and the Philippines, in 1898. There were pro-Allied and pro-German groups in the country, but no real question of entering the war arose. Her internal condition continued to decay. In 1923 the country seemed to be sliding into imminent ruin, and King Alfonso XIII entrusted General Primo de Rivera with dictatorial powers to pull it together. His dictatorship, mild and patriarchal, restored peace and stabilized the nation's economy. In the material sphere—roads, railways, public works and the like—he achieved wonders, and produced the same kind of results. At about the same period, as visitors to Italy universally recognized in the early years of Musso-lini's power there, efficiency, administrative honesty and cleanliness re-placed the ancient corruption. A regime, however, stands or falls by more than such exterior manifestations. Everybody may judge the Dictatorship for himself: how José Antonio, the Dictator's son, a son entirely devoted to his father, judged it, will be found in this book. We will merely record that José Antonio was never so much as a member of the General's "Unión Patriótica."

After the fall of General Primo de Rivera in 1930, the political situa-tion again became confused and full of unrest. Republicanism was rife, and on April 14th, 1931, King Alfonso formed the opinion that it was incumbent on him to retire from Spain—he did not abdicate—in order to avoid civil strife and bloodshed. The King and the Royal Family then left Spain, and the Republicans took power without any resistance.

This date, April 14th, 1931, is a cardinal one and must be borne care-fully in mind in order to appreciate a great many of the extracts in this book, and indeed a large proportion of José Antonio's thought in general. There are two main points in this connection which must be stressed. First, the Monarchy was not overthrown "constitutionally," so to speak, by any victory of a Republican party at a general election, at which the issue of Monarchy or Republic was before the electorate. There were, to be sure, Municipal Elections in progress, and many candidates were, in fact, persons of Republican opinions. The early results of these local gov-ernment polls, in Madrid and certain other large cities, returned a major-ity of councilors adhering to the Republican groups. The Monarch left Spain forthwith, without waiting even for the final results, which showed a large majority of Monarchist councilors over the country as a whole. Spain was thus faced with a situation surely without precedent in the history of monarchies: a King abandoned his realm in the middle of an election which lacked competence to express the people's will for him to go, and which in fact returned a majority of his supporters.

The second fact about April 14th, 1931, a fact continually referred to by José Antonio, is the *alegria*, as he calls it (light-heartedness, gaiety, cheerfulness) of the country as a whole. For the diehard Monarchists, it was of course a day of gloom and grief, aggravated by a number of Re-publican demonstrations of an extremist type. For out-and-out Republi-cans, it was a day of wild and even rowdy triumph. But José Antonio makes it clear that he is not referring to the latter, but to the cheerful air of anticipation that was abroad among the general mass, even among many who felt personally grieved to see the Monarchy fall. The date of April 14th, 1931 promised the Spanish people that at last "their revolu-tion" was going to be carried through; that is, the revolution towards so-cial justice. These bright expectations were not fulfilled.

This is not the place to pass judgment on the Republic, but simply to state its history. This falls into three phases: April 1931–November 1933, in which disappointment soon set in, the new rulers wasted their chances, laws against religion began to vex the Church, and the workers did not get their social justice. Spain began slipping down the slope again. November 1933–January 1936. In 1933 the Right Republican parties succeeded to power, at an election in which in many places only 40 percent of the electorate went to the polls. This reactionary period was equally sterile, but marked by even more serious events: the armed separatist rising of October 6th, 1934, in Catalonia, combined with a simultaneous Communist revolution in Asturias. Azaña, War Minister in the first Republican Government, and later the Popular-Front leader, was criminally implicated. This Government equally squandered its chances, and discontent grew into seething revolutionary feeling. The last phase, ushered in by the elections of February 1936. The Popular Front, with a minority of votes, aided by wholesale falsification of results and sheer violence, took power, bringing Azaña to office for the second time, as José Antonio had prophesied in a striking passage (Extract 165). Religious persecution, tyranny, and disorder of every kind at once broke out; churches, public buildings and newspaper offices were burnt, stormed and looted daily; murder was rife, starvation was widespread, public order ceased to exist. The Left extremists openly proclaimed the imminence of the Soviet revolution, which would have been an accomplished fact by the end of July. On July 12th, however, Calvo Sotelo, the Leader of the Parliamentary Opposition, who had been threatened with death in the Lobbies after his speeches exposing the tyranny of the regime, was "taken for a ride" by police officers on the instructions of the Government, and shot. His corpse was found lying at the cemetery gates next morning. This was the spark that fired the country. Four days later the Legion in Morocco rose against the Madrid Government; the attempts to murder Franco in Tenerife had failed, and he flew to North Africa in a small British aeroplane conveniently left unattended by Captain Pollard, V. C., acting under instructions from Douglas Jerrold. On the 18th of July 1936, the Spanish National Movement rose to anticipate by ten days the Communist revolution for which plans were now mature. The rest of the Republic's history is the history of the Spanish civil war, ending with the Nationalist victory of April 1st, 1939.

A phantom "government" lingered on, supported by that part of the Spanish national gold reserve which had not been given away to Russia; but any claim to legitimacy ever possessed by this body, on the strength of the dubious 1936 elections, finally ceased on July 6th, 1947, when the Spanish National Referendum on the Succession Bill gave official "democratic" sanction to Franco's regime and the constitution of Spain as a

Catholic Social Kingdom, wherein Franco, as unchallenged National Caudillo ("popular leader") will, in the course of time, be succeeded by either a King, or failing a suitable candidate of royal blood for the time being, by a Regent. It is interesting to note that this referendum, which passed off without the slightest incident of any kind and in perfect calm and good humor, showed a favorable vote which amounted to over 80 percent of the total electorate, vastly exceeding, in each single province without exception, the sum total of votes cast in 1936, not for the Popular Front alone, but for all the parties put together.

That is the framework of Spanish history in which José Antonio Primo de Rivera's short life was spent. He was born at Madrid in 1903, the eldest son of General Primo de Rivera. The family is an old Andalusian one from Jerez de la Frontera. The other children were two brothers, Miguel and Fernando, and two sisters, Carmen and Pilar. Miguel, who was not condemned to death at Alicante in 1936, has served Spain since the war as Minister of Agriculture and is at present (1947) serving as Mayor of Jerez, Fernando was murdered by the Marxists in Madrid, even before José Antonio wrote his will. Carmen is married and lives privately. Pilar, to whom this book is dedicated, is and always has been the National Delegate of the Feminine Section of the Falange. Her work in two directions especially has become famous: the training of Spanish womanhood at the Castillo de la Mota, Medina del Campo, and her successful labors, with her Section, in reviving and developing the vast resources of Spanish traditional folk-culture. A small sample of this latter was the appearance of the Spanish choirs and dancers at the 1947 Welsh Eisteddfod, which earned such remarkable tributes in Britain.

José Antonio read law and was called to the Bar as early as 1923. A recently published Spanish treatise on the philosophy of law[1] analyses his legal thought and describes him as one who would undoubtedly have won fame as a jurist had he lived in an age where his genius was not needed in politics. And indeed, even in his writings and speeches, although they deal with political subjects, it will be seen that he goes behind the forms that obsess all politicians and most statesmen, and is at grips with the inner essence or metaphysic, the changeless principles which are made manifest in various contingent spheres and at various levels in the universal hierarchy. To those acquainted with the metaphysical outlook, which must not be mistaken for philosophy, itself a very limited point of view, it will also prove interesting to note how José Antonio, even in the political sphere, envisages the cyclic theory in a micro-cosmic form, and how he foresees the cataclysm which may or may not be bridged when the cataclysm comes (that is, the barbarian invasion which

---

[1] "*Horizontes del pensamiento jurídico,*" by Luis Legaz y Lacambra, Professor of Philosophy of Law at Santiago University (Bosch, Barcelona, 1947).

is now not so much imminent as in process of consummation). Even in the period of darkness (Bolshevism) he can see the latent larvae of a new age, which it is Spain's mission to cherish for the world[2] into the fresh cycle to come.

His legal career was a brilliant one, while it lasted, but he soon found himself forced away from the intellectual life, which he loved, into the dust and heat of politics, which he did not. To be the son of the Dictator is a great handicap to a rising barrister. A would-be client once approached him with suggestions that his personal influence might well have a favorable effect on the Bench. In José Antonio's reply, which is extant, he forbids the "client" to enter his offices, threatening roundly to throw him downstairs if he presents himself with such aims in view. It would be pleasant to linger over many episodes in his non-political life, and to quote examples of his wit, his generosity, his charm, his "wholeness" as a man. But for these details a biography is needed; here, there is only space to speak of the Falange, its Founder, and how he quickened it by his death.

José Antonio had met Mussolini, and, like so many others, had been profoundly impressed by that remarkable genius. At the beginning of 1933 his mind appears to have entertained for some time the notion of a Spanish Fascism, and he even wrote an article for a projected periodical El Fascio, the director of which was a Conservative journalist with an inaccurate conception of what Fascism was. The paper was never born. The idea was immature and would certainly have failed in practice. No true Spaniard will knowingly follow a foreign model; the French influences and methods introduced under Bourbon monarchs have been uniformly disastrous; and, with memories of Charles V. and the "Great Captain," Spaniards would probably have been less amenable to Italian than to almost any other influence. Again, the Spanish view of life is profoundly theological, whereas Fascism, apart from its original work of restoring order out of chaos (purely nationalist and non-doctrinal) was a manifestation in the political sphere, and hence at a lower hierarchical level.

Sociologically, also, the Spanish national-syndicalist idea is very different from the Italian Corporativism, as will be clear from the appropriate passages in this book. And metaphysically, there could hardly be a more striking contrast than that between the Falange principles expressed in extracts 7, 10, 19, 59 and 62, among others, and the famous Fascist doctrine "All within the State, all for the State; none outside the State, none against the State." Even if in practice the resultant attitudes might from time to time coincide, the point of view is radically different, and

---

[2] See extract 75-77 especially.

the Spanish one is evidently attached to principles of a higher order. Lastly, there was a considerable Romantic element in the Italian movement (while German National-Socialism, in its plain outward form, was deeply imbued with Romanticism, a major component in most Germanic thought); and José Antonio was an uncompromising anti-Romantic. For the rest, the reader should refer to the text. He will see that José Antonio's observations about Fascism, most of which are taken from his letters to Luca de Tena, considerably antedate the foundation of the Falange. This event took place on October 29th, 1933, at a meeting held in the Comedy Theatre, Madrid. It is clear from the speech as a whole, and even from the extracts here quoted (which in fact amount to almost the whole of it, in sum) that José Antonio was setting forth a comprehensive doctrine which had long been crystallizing in his mind. There is no fumbling with ideas and no vagueness: all is clear-cut and decisive, like his own intellect.

However, if the doctrine appeared to spring forth, fully-armed like Athena from the head of Zeus, its embodiment in a practical movement was another matter, and the Falange as founded still lacked an essential part: the Syndical element, which was to do battle both physically and metaphysically for the soul of the working masses against the Marxian idea. This element, whose incorporation gave completeness to the movement, was added on February 13th, 1934, when the Falange and the J.O.N.S.[3] were fused into a single body. About the J.O.N.S. it is necessary to say a few words.

As early as 1931 similar doctrines and ideas, though differently expressed and addressed more particularly to the working masses, had assumed form. In February 1931, even before the fall of the Monarchy, Ramiro Ledesma Ramos had issued his Call to Youth, and a month later he published the first number of his journal Conquista del Estado. At Valladolid, in August of the same year, Onésimo Redondo founded the "Castilian Councils of Hispanic Action" and the paper Libertad. In November 1932 the two joined forces and chose as their emblem the Yoke and Arrows (taken from the coat-of-arms of Isabella the Catholic) and as their banner the red-and-black flag of the National Syndicate. This was the birth of the J.O.N.S., amalgamated in 1934 into the *Falange Española de las J.O.N.S.* under José Antonio's supreme leadership. There was yet another vital force in the country: living Traditionalism, represented by the Requetés; but they were far removed from the hubbub of parliamentary politics, and cherished their great Carlist traditions against the day when they might don the red beret once again and march forth from the fastnesses of Navarre to fight for God, King and Patria. Their day

---

[3] See Glossary.

came on July 18th, 1936. By July 20th they had already 20,000 armed and disciplined men in the field for General Mola, and they won the north for the national rising. This third great element was fused into the movement by General Franco on April 19th, 1937. All this, however, lay still unmanifested in the future, and does not directly touch the life of José Antonio. Nor have we space to speak further of the two great "Jonsistas" Ledesma and Redondo, beyond saying that they both gave their lives for the Movement as gallantly as their leader, the former only after a tragic lapse followed by reconciliation and atonement, in which he suffered murder and mutilation at the hands of the Marxist mob, the latter after an immaculate record of loyal service, in which he died fighting against odds in an ambush on his way to command the Falanges of the Castilian front in the early days of the civil war.

It is necessary to say a little about José Antonio as a member of Parliament. Nothing could have been more alien to his temperament and personal desires than such an occupation, as is evident from every reference he makes to the "inorganic" parliamentary system, its false assumptions and its futility. Circumstances, however, forced him to make use of it for the benefit of the cause he stood for. His first candidature was at a by-election in 1931, shortly after the Republic took over power. His sole object in standing was to defend the memory of his dead father, which was being slandered in every direction (see Extract 148). The constituency was a Madrid one and José Antonio stood as the candidate of the Right-wing bloc. Violent strikes and social conflicts had already broken out, and the first of the church-burnings had taken place on May 10th. José Antonio's Left-wing opponent received twice as many votes as he did, but it is noteworthy that he obtained 29,000 votes from electors who regarded him merely as the son of the dead and defamed Dictator.

He actually entered Parliament two years later. A month after the foundation of the Falange, in November 1933, at the end of the first two-year period of the Republic, he was returned as an Independent member for the province of Cadiz. What he thought of the system in general and of the Spanish Cortes of those days, the reader will see clearly enough. His presence in Parliament, however, was to be of the greatest service to the Falange, which he was able to defend against false (and sometimes criminal) accusations and misrepresentation, using the publicity of the House to defeat the general conspiracy of silence; and, still more, to advance his own doctrines, which were frequently adopted, in part, without acknowledgement, by politicians of various parties, including even Prieto (Extracts 265–267). Nevertheless, it would be quite incorrect to imagine that he merely used Parliament negatively and destructively; he frequently spoke on important affairs of state, having no direct connection with the Falange or its doctrines, and these speeches, models of statesmanship and dignity, stand out like jewels amid the mass of sterile twaddle that generally surrounds them in the parliamentary reports.

True to the Falange principle of upholding the national wellbeing against sectional vested interests, he refused to support an attempt to establish a sugar factory in his own constituency, as being prejudicial to the legitimate interests of other provinces and the nation. In the election when the Popular Front got power, this refusal caused the defection of many Right-wing voters who had helped to return him before. Their short-sighted and selfish attitude cost him his seat. This was little; but with the seat went parliamentary immunity from imprisonment, and the loss of this in the event meant the loss of his life.

With the advent of the Popular Front, a still fiercer persecution of the Falange began, with many murders and imprisonments, closing of branches and suppression of papers. He himself was arrested on a trumped-up charge in March 1936, and on one pretext or another was kept in detention till his death. All we have from March 1936 to the end consists of writings that he managed somehow to send secretly out of prison. First, there is the sheet of comments on current affairs and guidance for the Movement, written in what he calls the "horrifying underground dungeons" of Security-Police headquarters at Madrid ("Russia has been the real backer of the Popular Front, through the Communist party that she rules by her orders and her gold. Russia has won the elections").

Next, his Letter to the Army men of Spain, written from the Model Prison, Madrid. Then come three circulars of carefully thought-out instruction to local and national Falange leaders, warning them solemnly against certain traps and errors, especially the danger of becoming involved in a premature or unsound military rising. The last of these gives minute instructions how the Falange was to act in the case of such a rising, on receipt of orders from himself alone, and giving the watchword Covadonga—the name of the mountain cave, sacred to the Blessed Virgin, whence Pelayo the Goth initiated the first Reconquest of Spain for Christianity more than 1,200 years before. The first two are dated as from prison in Madrid and the dates are May 13th and June 24th. The third is dated June 29th and without place of origin, and its last line says that the instructions in it are to be deemed canceled on July 10th unless expressly renewed.

But by June 29th he was himself already in Alicante, whither he had been transferred on June 6th. He still managed to get a letter through, also dated June 29th, from the Alicante Provincial Prison, a sheet of cheer and encouragement to his "front-line comrades of Madrid."

In Alicante he was kept entirely incommunicado, with the solitary exception of the interview allowed to the reporter Jay Allen, of the London News Chronicle, an account of which was published in that paper on October 24th 1936. José Antonio refers to this interview in his Will, in which he speaks of the visit of "an American journalist." Readers of the News Chronicle will remember the ardent pro-Red sympathies of the paper; but a reference to the issue in question will show the astonishing impression made upon the reporter by José Antonio, some of whose words he has undoubtedly reported correctly. In particular, the following portion of the conversation is worth quoting[4]:

(Allen writes: "His eyes were fixed on me. He wanted news; he was longing for news. What could I tell him?" The Red guards of course, were standing by. "He anticipated me by saying:")

José Antonio—But what is happening now? I know nothing.

Allen—I am sure that these friends have not brought me here to give you information, but I will put some hypothetical questions which you can answer or not.

J. A.—All right.

A.—What would you think if I told you that my opinion is that General Franco's movement has left its original channel, whatever that was, and that from now on it is simply the old Spain fighting for lost privileges?

J. A.—I know nothing, but I do not believe it is true. If it is, it is wrong.
A.—And if I told you that your men are fighting in the service of the landlords?

J. A.—I should tell you they are not. J. A. (Continuing.)—Do you remember my position and my speeches in the Cortes? You know I said that if after October 1934 the Right-wing kept on with their negative policy of repression, Azaña would be back in power very soon. The same would happen now. If all they are doing is putting back the clock, they are mistaken. They will not be able to master Spain if that is all they are doing. I stood for

---

[4] The following words may not tally verbatim with the newspaper, since they are translated from the Spanish records which were made in halite on the battlefield, but the sense is the same.

something different, something positive. You have read the program of our national-syndicalism, the agrarian reform and all our aims. I was sincere. I could have become a Communist and achieved popularity.

J. A.—I know that if this movement wins and proves to be merely reactionary, I will then retire, with the Falange, and I—I shall be in this or some other prison in a few months' time.

("He seemed full of extraordinary confidence," wrote Allen, adding: "Yes, it was a magnificent bluff!")

Allen. (to the Red guards.)—What are you going to do with him?

Guards.—There'll be a trial. (They looked at one another.)

(Allen concludes: "I cannot in any way imagine any circumstances that could save this young man. His situation is very grave. The least I can do is not to make it worse.")

Two writings remain: his Last Manifesto and his Will. Both are quoted in full in this book and require no comment, except on one small point.

Why was he sent to Alicante? In his Will he makes some obscure allusions, the only vagueness noticeable in his crystalline style. There were many plans concocted for rescuing him: some completely harebrained, such as the bright idea of sending the gigantic pugilist Paulino Uzcudun, the Basque woodcutter, to Alicante to break into the prison by force: others merely wild, and one or two which might well have succeeded but for a chance recognition. But Alicante was not the original place to which it was intended to send him. Had the original plan been followed, a rescue could in all likelihood have been affected. It is known that the plans were changed at the last moment, and José Antonio may have believed that this was done in order to make his death certain. In fact, there are grounds for believing that the Government official who made the change did so in the honest belief that he was rendering a rescue less unlikely and not more. Both are dead now, and there is no more to be said. But this may serve to explain that curious passage in his Will.

This book is an anthology of his thought, and not a biographical work, still less a panegyric. It is not the place to speak of the manner in which he met his death, beyond giving the bare facts.

He was tried on November 19th, together with his brother Miguel and his sister-in-law Margot. He defended himself and them, calm and un-moved, in a speech which the Red newspaper El Día, of Alicante, de-scribes as "a masterpiece of forensic oratory, which the public listened to with rapt attention and obvious interest." At the end of it, the journal-ists conversed shortly with him, and the same newspaper records his last words spoken in public:

"You will see now that no ideological gulfs separate us; if we men knew one another and talked to one another, we should realize that these gulfs we think we see are nothing but little valleys." Then came the hours of waiting for the verdict; finally, the sentence.

It happened, by an amazing chance, that a fellow-prisoner was a priest, to whom José Antonio was allowed access that he might be shriven. At dawn on the 20th of November, he bade farewell to his brother and was taken out into a courtyard to be shot. Prophetically an-ticipating the future plenitude of the movement he created, he stood to face the rifles with two Falangists on one side and two Requetés on the other. He gave a lusty cry of "Arriba España" and kissed the crucifix in humility. A moment later his body was dead.

That body now lies in a tomb before the High Altar of the Basilica of the Escorial, to which it was conveyed by thousands of Spaniards who carried the coffin on foot from Alicante. Franco has said:

"Spaniards: José Antonio has died, the newscriers say. José Antonio lives, the Falange declares. What is death and what is life . . . ? Life is immortality. . . . The seed that is not lost, but day after day is renewed with new vigor and freshness. . . . This is the life, today, of José Anto-nio."

Sonnet to José Antonio

by DIONISIO RIDRUEJO

El rastro de la Patria, fugitivo
en el aire, sin sales ni aventura,
fue arrebatado en fuego por la altura
de su ágil corazón libre y cautivo.
De la costra del polvo primitivo
alzó la vena de su sangre pura,
trenzando con el verbo su atadura
de historia y esperanza en pulso vivo.
Enamoró la luz de las espadas,
armó las almas sin albergue, frías;
volvió sed a las aguas olvidadas.
Dió raíz a la espiga y a la estrella
y, por salvar la tierra con sus días,
murió rindiendo su hermosura en ella.

His country's trail that wandered wearily
aimless in air, sans wit, sans enterprise,
was swept in rapture as a flame that flies
by that swift-soaring heart, captive and free.
Out of the dust where it had lain so long
the pure heroic vein he disinterred,
weaving its live connection with the Word
of history and hope, pulsating strong.
Captive in love he led the swordblades gleam,
rearmed the chilled and homeless souls of men
gave thirst anew where waters lay forlorn,
roots to the star and to the ear of corn,
and, that his span of days might earth redeem,
died, yielding up his beauty in her again.

TRANSLATOR'S NOTE

The version has been made as exact as possible both as to meaning and even, where practicable, style also. The numeration of the extracts corresponds to that of the original Spanish edition, with the exceptions noted in the concordance. In about a dozen instances, substitution, has been thought advisable; the object has been to replace pieces which are of great interest and importance to Spaniards only, by others of approximately similar thought which are of more interest to English-speaking readers. In addition, three or four pieces of exceptional significance today have been substituted for others whose application is less universal or less topical. In doing this, pains have been taken to interfere to the minimum extent with the development of the logical train of thought that has governed the anthologist in his selection and arrangement of the extracts. One or two references omitted in the Spanish edition have been inserted; each reference has been given in full and dated, instead of being denoted by initials only as in the Spanish; and occasionally one or two extra words, or a sentence, from the original have been added to, or included in, a given extract when this seemed necessary to make the context clearer to the English-speaking reader.

The Last Manifesto of José Antonio, written the day before the National Rising, and his Will, written thirty-six hours before his death, have been added as a supplement.

Madrid, July 1947

GLOSSARY

C. E. D. A : (*Confederación Española de Derechas Autónomas*). Right-wing bloc of parties under the leadership of Gil Robles.

Cortes : The Spanish national Parliament.

Generalidad : The autonomous Parliament of the region of Catalonia, which in fact tended towards separatism, to the point of actual armed rebellion (against the Republic) in 1934.

J. O. N. S. : (*Juntas de Ofensiva Nacional-Sindicalistas*). National-syndicalist councils of action. The movement which started a little before the *Falange Española*. After a short period of independent life, the two movements were fused into the single movement of *Falange Española de las J.O.N.S.* The occasion of the fusion was marked by the Valladolid meeting of 4-3-24. The aims of the two original movements were identical although the angle of approach was not always the same. The Falange (F.E. de las J.O.N.S.) continued with this title until it and the Requeté movement (the heir to the Carlists), of patriotic and Traditionalist aims, were incorporated together by General Franco, as Head of the Nationalist Movement, in 1937, under the comprehensive title of *Falange Española Tradicionalista y de las J.O.N.S.* which it bears today.

Jurados mixtos : Joint Courts of employers and employees for settling industrial and labor disputes.

Populist : A word to denote the attitude of *Accion Popular*, a subsection of the C. E. D. A.

Puerta del Sol : The 'heart' of Madrid, corresponding to Piccadilly Circus in London.

S. E. U. : (*Sindicato Español Universitario*). The syndicate, or guild, of University students.

Syndicate : correctly, vertical syndicates. Rather 'guild' than 'trade-union', since the latter normally includes employees alone. The vertical syndicate runs through each branch of production or other economic-social activity, from bottom to top, including manual workers, intellectual workers, technicians, management and shareholders (if any), i.e. all elements that make a contribution to the national welfare in this branch of activity. Hence, the notion of class-struggle or opposition can have no place. The syndical aim is that all of these elements shall not merely enjoy representation but participate proportionately in the control and profits of the undertaking. The difference between this national-syndicalist system and the early class-syndicalism (e.g. in Italy), and on the other hand between this system of vertical guilds and the 'corporative state' will be clearly apparent.

PART ONE

DOCTRINE

PART ONE: DOCTRINE

I.

INTELLECTUAL FOUNDATIONS

1.   As we stand beside this milestone on our road, with our face set towards History, a strict conciseness of language and attitude is demanded of us.

Speech, Madrid, 19-5-35.

2.   The Good and the True are permanent categories of right reason, and to find out if one is right, it is not enough to enquire of the king—whose will, in the eyes of partisans of absolute monarchy, was always just; nor is it enough to enquire of the people—whose will, in the eyes of Rousseau's followers, is always correct; but at every instant we must see whether our acts are in accord with a permanent aim and object.

Parliament, 19-12-33.

3.   [I]t is possible to attain to enthusiasm and love by way of the intelligence.

Ibid., 3-7-34.

4.   The heart has its reasons which the reason does not comprehend. But the intelligence also has its own manner of loving, such as perhaps the heart is unaware of.

Essay on Nationalism, April 1934.

5.   The unimpassioned interplay of laws is always surer than our individual understanding, just as the balance weighs more accurately than our hand.

Lecture, "Law and Politics," 11-11-35.

II.

THE CONCEPTION OF MAN

6.   We regard the individual as the fundamental unity, because that is the feeling of Spain, which has always regarded man as a bearer of eternal values.

Speech, "Spain and Barbarism," Valladolid, 3-3-35.

7.   [T]he liberty of man is only respected when he is considered, as we consider him, as the bearer of eternal values; when he is considered as the corporeal envelope of a soul capable of damnation or of salvation. Only when he is thus considered can it be said that his liberty is truly respected. . . .

Speech, Madrid, 29-10-33.

8.   The Individual bears the same relation to the Person as the People bears to the Political Society.

9.   Nobody is "one" except in so far as there can exist "others." What makes us Persons is not our individual physical equipment, but the existence of others whose being also "persons" differentiates us.

"F.E.," 7-12-33.

10.   [T]he true juridical reality is the "person"; that is, the individual, regarded not from his own point of view as a living reality, but as an active or passive bearer of social relations which are governed by the Law; as capable of making demands, being coerced, attacking and transgressing.

Essay on Nationalism, April 1934.

11.   One is only a "person" in so far as one is "another"; that is, one as against the others, a potential creditor or debtor with regard to the others, a holder of positions that are not those of others. The personality, then, is not determined from within by being an aggregate of cells, but from without, by being a bearer of relations.

Ibid.

12.   Nobody was ever born a member of a political party; on the contrary, we are all born members of one family; we are all citizens of one Municipality; we all press forward in the exercise of one task of work.

Speech, Madrid, 29-10-33.

13.   Only when service is given is human dignity attained. Only he is great who binds himself down to filling a place in the achievement of a great undertaking. This essential point, the greatness of the end aspired to, is what you are not willing to take into consideration.

2nd Open Letter to Luca de Tena, "ABC," 23-3-33.

14.   The "young gentleman" is the degeneration of the "gentleman," the "hidalgo," who wrote until very recently the finest pages in as much

as he was capable of "renouncing," that is, giving up privileges, comfort and pleasures, in order to honor a lofty ideal of "service." Noblesse oblige, was what the gentlemen, the hidalgos, thought; that is to say, nobility "demands" it. The more one is, the more one has to be capable of omitting to be. And so it was from those who were models of the hidalgo that most of the names emerged which won laurels in sacrifice.

"Señoritismo," "F.E.," 25-1-34.

15.   Consider what European man has become reduced to by the action of capitalism. He has no longer a house, he has no longer an individuality, he has no longer a craftsman's ability; he is now merely a number of conglomerations.

Speech, Madrid, 19-5-35.

16.   [T]he characteristic feature of the Spanish tragedy and the European tragedy . . . (is this): man has been disintegrated, uprooted, transformed . . . into a number on the electoral roll and a number in the queue at the factory gates; what this disintegrated man is crying out for is to feel the ground under his feet again, to be put in harmony once more with a collective destiny, a common destiny, or simply—calling things by their right names—with the destiny of his Patria.

Lecture, Madrid, 9-4-35.

17.   In the city you hardly see the man. He is always concealed behind his job, behind his clothes. In the city you see the merchant, the electrician, the lawyer, and so on. In the country you always see the man.

"Go to the Country."

18.   Those of us who go from the city into the country always feel a little inferior in the presence of the people there, who can barely discern us amid the clothing.

Ibid.

19.   When the world is off its hinges, it cannot be put to rights by technical patching: it needs a complete new order. And this order must once again spring from the individual.

Speech, "Spain and Barbarism," Valladolid, 3-3-35.

III.
HUMAN FREEDOM

20.   In face of Lenin's contemptuous "Freedom, what for?" we begin by affirming the freedom of the individual and by recognizing the individual. We who have been maligned as advocates of State Pantheism, begin by accepting the reality of the free individual, the bearer of eternal values.

Lecture, "State, Individual, Freedom," 28-3-35.

21.   Man must be free, but freedom does not exist except within an order.

Speech, "Spain and Barbarism," Valladolid, 3-3-35.

IV.
PROPERTY AND LABOR
AS ELEMENTARY HUMAN ATTRIBUTES

22.   Property is the direct projection of man upon his goods; it is an elementary human attribute. Capitalism has been replacing this property of man by the property of capital, by the technical instrument of economic domination.

Speech, Madrid, 19-5-35.

23.   Labor is a human function, just as property is a human attribute. What is all this about harmonizing capital with Labor?

Speech, "Spain and Barbarism," Valladolid, 3-3-35.

V.
CONCEPT OF LIFE

24.   The religious and the military are the only two complete and serious modes of understanding life.

Speech, Madrid, 17-11-35.

25.   All human existence—of individuals or nations—is a tragic struggle between the automatic urge and that which is hard work.

Essay on Nationalism, April 1934.

26.   The spiritual positions thus captured in heroic struggle against the automatic urge are those which later on become the deepest foundations of what is genuine in us.

Ibid.

27.   Such, amongst others, is the sweet recompense that is won by the effort at improvement: elementary joys may perhaps be lost, yet others are waiting at the end of the road, others so dear and so keen that they even invade the sphere of the old affections, which fade away at the outset of the undertaking that overrides them.

Ibid.

VI.
PEOPLE

28.   [A] people is . . . a single integer of destiny, effort, sacrifice and struggle, which must be considered as a whole, marches through history as a whole, and must be served as a whole.

Parliament, 19-12-33.

VII.
HISTORY

29.   The life of all peoples is a tragic struggle between the automatic and the historic. Peoples in a primitive state are able to feel the characteristics of the soil in an almost vegetative way. When they transcend this primitive state, peoples realize that they are molded not by the characteristics of the soil, but by the mission that differentiates them from others amid universality. When the decadent stage in this sense of universal mission is reached, separatisms begin to flourish once more, and once more people begin to go back to their own soil, their own music, their own dialect, and once more that glorious integrity, which was the Spain of the great days, is placed in jeopardy.

Speech, Valladolid, 4-3-34.

30.   A complete interpretation of history and politics, as I said at the meeting in the Comedy Theatre, is like the law of love: one must possess an understanding of love, which without written program or numbered sections and paragraphs will tell us at any given instant when we must embrace and when we must quarrel.

Speech, Madrid, 2-2-36.

31.   That we are witnessing the end of an epoch is a fact that practically no-one, unless he has an axe to grind, will dare to deny. This epoch which is now in its death-throes has been a short one and a brilliant. Its birth may be placed in the third decade of the eighteenth century; its internal motive power might be expressed in the single word: Optimism. The nineteenth century, developing as it did under the tutelary shades of Adam Smith and Rousseau, really believed that by leaving things to run themselves everything would turn out for the best both in the political and the economic order.

Tradition and Revolution, Aug. 1935.

32.   Our times grant no quarter. Our lot has been a warlike one, in which we may spare neither our skin nor our heart's blood. In obedience to our destiny we travel from place to place, enduring the shame of appearing like a public show; obliged to shout aloud things we have thought out in the austerest silence; suffering distortion at the hands of those who do not and those who will not understand us; breaking our backs in this ridiculous sham, this procedure of winning over "public opinion"—as if the people, capable as it is of love or anger, were collectively susceptible of opinion.

"Haz," 5-12-35.

33.   All young men conscious of their responsibility are pressing for the reform of the world. They are pressing forward on the path of action, and, which is more important on that of thought, without whose constant supervision all action is mere barbarism. We could ill afford to stand aside from this universal concern, we men of Spain for whom the days of our youth opened in the perplexities of the post-war years.

Tradition and Revolution, Aug. 1935.

34.   We, the young, who are stirred by spiritual urges, free from the crude selfishness of the old political bosses—what we have been seeking is a Spain having greatness and justice, an order and a faith.

"Arriba," 7-11-35.

35.   What are they waiting for now, the young men out in the cold? Shall they give up all hope? Shall they retire to the ivory towers? Shall they wait, and put their trust anew in party cries, once more to seduce them and once more to bring disillusion?

Ibid.

VIII.
PATRIA AND PATRIOTISM

36.   The Patria is that which is bodied forth as a great collective undertaking. If there is no undertaking there is no Patria; without the presence of faith in a common destiny, the whole thing fades away into native scenery, into local tastes and colors.

Bagpipe and Lyre, "F.E.," 11-1-34,

37.   The Patria is a complete unit, in which all individuals and all classes are integrated; the Patria cannot remain in the hands of the most powerful class or of the best organized party. The Patria is a transcendent synthesis, an individual synthesis, with ends of its own to achieve.

Speech, Madrid, 29-10-33.

38.   A dream of unity and a common task, as against the narrow particularism and retrogression of the suicidal disintegrations.

Exhortation to Catalonia.

39.   The Patria is the only possible collective destiny. If we reduce it to something smaller, say to the home or the plot of ground, then we are left with an almost physical relationship alone; if we extend it to the world, we get lost in a conception too vague to be grasped. It is exactly the Patria which on a physical basis forms a differentiation in the universal order; it is precisely that which binds together, and at the same time differentiates within the universal order, the destiny of a whole people; it is, as we always say, a unity of destiny within the Universal.

Lecture, Madrid. 9-4-35.

40.   We want the Patria to be understood as a harmonic indivisible reality, above all conflicts of individuals, classes, parties and natural differences.

41.   A Patria that is clear-cut, light-footed, enterprising, wiped clean of the smear of brass-band jingoism and of many a crust of inveterate filth. Not a Patria to be extolled in stodgy effusions, but to be understood and felt as the executrix of a great destiny.

42.   Patria, meaning not merely the soil upon which a number of rival parties cut one another to pieces—even though only with the weapons of invective—in their ambition for power. Nor the field in which the everlasting conflict unfolds between a bourgeoisie trying to exploit the proletariat and a proletariat trying to tyrannize over the bourgeoisie. Not

these, but the heartfelt unity of all in the service of a historic mission, a supreme communal destiny, which allots to each man his task, his rights, and his sacrifices.

Open Letter to Luca de Tena. "ABC." 23-3-33.

43.   Spain is more than a constitutional form. . . . Spain is more than a historical circumstance. . . . Spain can never be anything which is in opposition to the aggregate of her lands and to each individual one of them.

Parliament, 2-1-34.

44.   Spain, not as an empty invocation of inflated shams, but as a complete expression of a spiritual and human content: Patria, bread, and Justice.

45.   Spain, since her existence began, has meant and always will mean a job to be done. . . . Spain is only justified by having a mission to fulfil. . . . Spain cannot be given over to unending seasons of leisure, shallowness, and lack of vital purpose.

Parliament, 25-1-35.

46.   Spain's justification is an imperial vocation to unite languages, to unite races, to unite peoples, and to unite customs in one universal destiny.

47.   Spain is "irrevocable." Spaniards may make decisions on secondary things; but as to the essence of Spain itself there is nothing for them to decide. Spain is "ours," as an heirloom is ours: our generation is not the absolute owner of Spain: she has come down to them from the efforts of generations and generations in the past, and she must be handed on like a sacred deposit, to the generations to come. If our generation took advantage of this moment of its own passing presence amid the continuity of the centuries in order to split Spain into fragments, our generation would be committing the most abominable fraud and most perfidious treason that it is possible to imagine against those who are to follow.

Bagpipe and Lyre, "F.E.," 11-1-34.

48.   If patriotism were a matter of tenderness of affection, it would not be the highest of human loves. Man's patriotism would be inferior to that of the plants, which surpass him in their clinging to the soil. The name of patriotism cannot be given to the first component of our nature that we come upon, namely that primordial impregnation with the earthy element. Patriotism—if it is to achieve its highest degree—must be that

which lies absolutely at the opposite extreme; that which is most difficult; that which is most purged of earthy drosses; that which is sharpest
and clearest-cut; that which is most unchanging. In other words: its stan-
chions must be sunk not in the feelings but in the intellect.

Bagpipe and Lyre, "F.E.," 11-1-34.

49.   [T]here is no fertile patriotism except what comes by the way
of criticism. And I will tell you that our own patriotism too has come by
the way of criticism. We are not stirred to either a greater or a lesser
degree by that musical-comedy patriotism which rejoices in the present-
day mediocrities and paltrinesses of Spain and in heavy interpretations
of the past. We love Spain because we find her unattractive. Those who
love their country because they find her attractive love her with a will
towards contact, they love her physically, sensually. We love her with a
will towards perfection. It is not this ruin, this decay of our physical
Spain of today that we love. What we love is the eternal and changeless
metaphysic of Spain.

Speech, Madrid, 19-5-35.

50.   This type of patriotism is harder to feel: but in its difficulty lies
its greatness. . . . Just as patriotism towards one's native earth is felt
without any effort, or even with a toxic and sensual pleasure, it is a fine
human undertaking to escape from its toils and rise above it into the patriotism of the hard, intellectual mission. Such will be the task of a new
nationalism: to replace the feeble attempt to combat Romantic movements with Romantic weapons, by resolutely erecting strong, classical,
impregnable redoubts against the floods of Romanticism; by sinking the
foundations of patriotism not in emotional but in intellectual ground; by
causing patriotism to be not a vague feeling that withers with the least
inconstancy of will, but a truth as unshakable as the truths of mathemat-
ics. This does not mean that patriotism will be no more than an arid product of the intellect.

Essay on Nationalism, April 1934.

IX.
THEORY OF THE NATION

51.   The nation is not a geographical reality, nor a racial, nor a linguistic one; it is essentially a historical unity. An aggregation of men
upon a piece of ground is only a nation in so far as it is a function of the
universal, if it fulfils a destiny of its own in History, a destiny which is

not that of "the rest." "The rest" are always those by whom we tell that we are "one."

In the common life which I share with men, I am he who is not any of the others. In the universal common life, each nation is that which none of the others is. Hence, nations are determined from without; they are distinguished from the environment amidst which they fulfil their own, and universal, destiny.

"F.E.," 7-12-33.

52.   We realize that a nation is not merely the attractive force of the soil on which we are born, it is not that direct sentimental emotion that we all feel in the presence of our own earth, but a nation is a unity of destiny in the universal order, it is a plane to which a people has risen when it fulfils a universal mission in History. . . .

Parliament, 4-1-34.

53.   Nations are not "contracts" that can be rescinded at the will of those who enter into them; they are "foundations" with a proper substantiality of their own, not dependent on the will of the many or of the few.

54.   From now on, for clearness sake, it will be convenient to use the word "nation," meaning by that word precisely this: the political society capable of finding its machinery of operation in the State. Thus, the theme of the present essay stands defined: to explain what the nation is; whether it is the spontaneous reality of a people, as the Romantic nationalists think, or whether it is something not determined by natural characteristics.

Essay on Nationalism, April 1934.

55.   The Romantic thesis was aimed at "disqualification," that is, at the abolition of all elements such as Law and History added as a result of effort to the primitive entities of individual and people. Law had transformed the "individual" into a "person"; History had transformed the "people" into the "polis," into the political condition of a State. . . . For the Romantic thesis it was a matter of vital interest to return to the primitive, to the spontaneous, in either case.

Ibid.

56.   Romanticism is a frail attitude which seeks precisely to lay basic foundations on swampy soil; Romanticism is a school of thought with no hard and fast lines, which at each moment and in each crisis entrusts the Sensitive faculty with the solution of those problems which should only be entrusted to the reason.

Parliament, 3-7-34.

57.   Romanticism had a leaning towards naturism. The "return to nature" was its watchword. Thus, the "nation" came to be identified with that which was "native." The things that determined a nation were the ethnical, linguistic, geographical, and climatic characteristics. In the limiting case, community of usages, customs, and tradition; but the word tradition is to be taken as little more than the remembrance of the same reiterated usage, and not in any reference to a historical process that should be like a starting point towards a perhaps unattainable objective. The most dangerous nationalisms, for their disintegrative effect, are those which have envisaged the nation in this manner. If it be granted that the nation is determined by the spontaneous element, the particularist nationalisms achieve an impregnable position. Undoubtedly the spontaneous element is in accord with this view. That is why it is so easy to feel local patriotism. That is why peoples get so readily lit up by the joyous rapture of their own songs, their own festivals, their own soil. In all this there is something like a sensuous appeal, which can be perceived even in the smell of the earth; a physical, primordial, warming and quickening current, something akin to drunkenness or to the fullness of plants in the period of fertilization.

It is to this rustic and primitive condition that nationalisms of Romantic type owe their extreme brittleness.

Nothing angers men and peoples more than to find obstacles in the path of their most elementary urges: hunger and sex—appetites of an order analogous to the dim call of the earth—are capable, if unsatisfied, of unleashing the gravest tragedies. . . .

When one of these primordial feelings implanted in the depths of a people's instinct is offended, their elemental reaction in an opposite direction is inevitable, even on the part of those least wedded to the nationalist spirit. It is almost a question of a biological phenomenon.

Not much brighter, however, is the attitude of those who, when confronted with the feeling of localistic patriotism, have been straining hard for the direct awakening of a merely unitarian patriotic feeling. Sentiment for sentiment, the simplest always prevails. When unitary patriotism descends to the plane of sensation, perceptible by an almost vegetable consciousness, the nearer it is the more intense it becomes.

How, then, is the patriotism of the large, heterogeneous units to be revived? By nothing less than revising the idea of the "nation" in order to set it up on a different footing. And here we may employ as our rule what has been said regarding the difference between the "individual" and the "person." Just as the person is the individual regarded as a function of society, so the nation is the people regarded as a function of the universal order.

The Person is not so designated qua dark or fair, tall or short, a speaker of this or that language, but qua bearer of such and such definitely regulated social relationships. One is only a Person in so far as one is "another"; that is, one as against the Others, a potential creditor or debtor with regard to others, a holder of positions that are not those of the others. The Personality, then, is not determined from within by being an aggregate of cells, but from without, by being a bearer of relations. In the same way, a people is not a nation by virtue of any kind of physical qualification, by local colors or favors, but by "being Other in the universal order"; that is to say, by having a destiny which is not that of the other nations. Thus, not every people or aggregate of peoples is a nation, but only those ones which fulfil a historic destiny differentiated in the universal order.

Accordingly, it is superfluous to investigate whether a nation furnishes the prerequisites of geographical, racial or linguistic unity; what matters is to discover whether it possesses, in the universal order, this unity of historic destiny.

The classical ages saw this with their usual clarity. That is why they never used the words "patria" and "nation" in the Romantic sense, or anchored patriotism to a dim love of the soil. Rather did they prefer expressions having an allusion to the "historic instrument." The word "Spain," which in itself connotes an Undertaking, will always possess much more significance than the phrase "the Spanish nation." In England, which is perhaps the country having the most classic patriotism of all, not only the word "patria," does not exist, but there are few people capable of distinguishing the word "King," the symbol of the unity operating throughout their history, from the word "country," which is a reference to the territorial basis of that unity itself.

We have reached the end of our journey. It is only when thus understood that a nation's patriotism can prevail over the disintegrative effect of local nationalisms. Everything genuine that the latter contain must be recognized; but in face of them it is necessary to arouse a vigorous movement of aspiration towards the nationalism which is missionary, and which conceives the Patria as a historic unity of destiny.

Essay on Nationalism, April 1934.

X.

THE STATE

58.   We want the State to be always an instrument at the service of a historic destiny, at the service of a historic mission of unity; we reckon that the State is behaving well if it believes in this complete historical destiny, if it regards the people as an integrated total of aspirations, because we realize that that is what a people is: a single integer of destiny, effort, sacrifice and struggle, which must be considered as a whole, marches through History as a whole, and must be served as a whole.

Parliament, 19-12-33.

59.   We consider that the conduct of a State, just like that of an individual or a class, is justified, at any given moment, only in so far as it conforms at each moment to an unchanging rule or norm.

Parliament, 19-12-33.

60.   [W]hat is this business of a strong State? A State may be strong when it serves a great destiny, when it feels itself to be the instrument of a great destiny for a people. Otherwise the State is tyrannical.

Lecture, Madrid, 9-4-35.

61.   [T]he only State which can be strong without being tyrannical is one that serves a unity of destiny. That is how the strong State, as servant of the consciousness of unity, is the real guarantee of the individual's liberty. On the other hand, the State which does not feel itself to be the servant of one supreme unity is always afraid of being regarded as tyrannous.

Speech, "Spain and Barbarism," Valladolid, 3-3-35.

62.   The deification of the State is the exact opposite of what we desire.

Parliament, 19-12-33.

63.   [I]t is a false point of view which sets the individual in opposition to the State and conceives their respective sovereignties as antagonistic. This idea "sovereignty" has cost the world much blood and will cost it more. For in this sovereignty lies the principle that legitimizes any action merely by virtue of its author's being who he is. Naturally, as against the Sovereign's right to do what he likes, the right of the individual to do what he likes will be raised in opposition. The case is thus insoluble. . . .   Lecture, "State, Individual, Freedom," 4-4-35.

64.   The State entrenches itself behind its sovereignty, and the individual behind his; both fight for the right to do as they please. The case has no solution. But there is a just and a fruitful issue to this conflict if it is envisaged from a different standpoint. That destructive antagonism disappears in proportion as the problem of the individual as against the State can be conceived not as a competition between powers and between rights, but as one of fulfilment of purposes and destinies. The Patria is a "unity of destiny in the universal order," and the individual is the holder of a mission all his own within the harmony which is the State. Here there is no room for disputes of any kind; the State cannot be false to its task nor can the individual fail to be a collaborator in his, in the perfect order of the nation's life. . . .

The idea of "destiny" that which provides justification for the existence of an edifice (State or system), informed the loftiest age ever enjoyed by Europe: the thirteenth century, the century of St. Thomas. And it was born in the mind of friars. The friars looked the power of kings in the face, and denied them it in so far as it should not be justified by the fulfilment of a great end. . . .

If we accept this definition of the Being—the holder of a mission, the unit that fulfils a destiny—there blossoms forth the noble, great, robust conception of "service." If no one exists save as an executor of a task, then precisely personality, unity and liberty themselves are attained by "serving" in the total harmony. . . . Nobody feels himself duplicated, dissected, or self-contradictory, as between what he is in reality and what he represents in public life.

The individual, then, takes part in the State as one fulfilling a function, and not through the medium of the political parties; not as the representative of a false sovereignty, but by virtue of having a job and a family, by virtue of belonging to a Municipality. Thus, a man is at once a diligent executive and a depositary of the Power. . . .

The State, the synthesis of so many fruitful activities, looks to its universal destiny. And as the Leader is he to whom the highest magistracy has been entrusted, it is he who serves most. Coordinator of the multiplicity of particular destinies, helmsman controlling the course of the great ship of the Patria, he is the "First Servant"; he is, like him who incarnates the highest magistracy on earth "the slave of the slaves of God."

Ibid.

XI.

POLITICS

65.   If political thought is not exacting in its approaches to problems—in other words, strict in the intellectual order—it will probably amount to no more than a heavy wing-flapping upon the surface of the mediocre.

Tribute and Reproach to Ortega, "Haz," 5-12-35.

66.   Political thought is, above all, temporal. Politics is a game played against Time in which not a single move may legitimately be postponed. In politics there is an obligation to arrive, and to arrive on time.

Ibid.

67.   No regime can endure if it does not succeed in rallying around it the generation which is young at the moment of its own birth, and in order to rally the young generation it is essential to find the right words, to hit on the right formula of ideological expression.

Parliament, 6-6-34.

68.   When one reaches a political position by this somewhat dramatic path that I had to follow, this path on which I have had to endure many sufferings in the most intimate portion of my sensibility, one does not come forth into the outer world and abandon one's peace of mind, profession, normal way of life and chances of cultivating the things of the mind and living away from the noise, in that silence out of which the only really fruitful work emerges; one does not leave all that behind, I say, merely to have pleasure of raising one's arm in here. One does it because our generation, which has perhaps thirty or forty years of life before it, will not resign itself once more to continue living in that flat layer of existence bounded respectively by absence of historical interest and absence of social justice.

Ibid.

69.   One must believe in something. When has anyone got anywhere with a liberal point of view? The only fruitful cases, frankly, that I am aware of have come from the politics of belief, in one sense or another.

When a State lets itself be won over to the conviction that nothing is good or evil and that its only duty is that of a policeman, that State perishes at the first warm blast of positive belief, in a series of municipal elections.

1st Open Letter to Luca de Tena, "ABC." 22-3-33.

70.   All great political thought relies on the coming to birth of a great faith. Looking outwards from within—on the People, or on History—the statesman's function is a religious and poetical one. The lines of communication between the leader and his people are no longer merely intellectual, but poetical and religious. It is precisely in order that a people may not become watery or amorphous—may not lose its backbone—that the masses must follow their leaders as they would prophets. This interpenetration of the mass by the leaders is attained by a process similar to that of love.

Hence the tremendous seriousness of the moment when one accepts a post of captaincy. Merely by taking it on, one assumes the vast and unescapable responsibility of revealing to a people—which as a mass is incapable of making the discovery by itself—where its real destiny lies. He who correctly strikes the first note, in the mysterious music of each age, cannot now excuse himself from finishing the melody. He now carries with him a whole people's hopes, and the tremendous account has been opened, the account of his stewardship in regard to them. What a responsibility will be his, if, as in Browning's poem, he draws a childlike crowd after him with his piping, only to bury them beneath a mountain from which there is no return!

Tribute and Reproach to Ortega, "Haz," 5-12-35.

71.   There has been kindled in Europe, and there now burns in Spain, the fire of a new faith. A faith which in the earthly and civil order, sees this as a primary truth: that a people is a total, indivisible, living entity, with a destiny of its own to fulfil in the universal order. The welfare of each one of those who integrate the people is not an individual interest but a collective one, with which the community, is bound to concern itself as being unequivocally and in the deepest sense its own. No private interest is foreign to the interest of the community, and accordingly it is not legitimate for anyone to shoot away the foundations of the community out of private interest, intellectual caprice, or pride.

New Light in Spain, May 1934.

72.   There is the task of our times: to restore to men the ancient savors of Law and of Bread; to get them to see that law and order is better than license; that even occasional indulgence in license implies the certainty that a return to fixed moorings is possible. And on the other hand, in the economic order, to get man to feel the ground under his feet again, to bind him in a deeper sense to his things—the home he lives in and the daily work of his hands.

Tradition and Revolution, August 1935.

73.   The man is the system; this is one of the deep human truths which Fascism has made effective again. The whole of the nineteenth century was wasted in thinking out machinery for good government. This is about as useful as trying to discover a thinking—machine or a loving-machine. Nothing genuine, permanent and difficult, such as governing, has ever been capable of being done by machinery; it has always been necessary in the end to have recourse to that which from the beginning of the world has been the one and only apparatus capable of guiding men: the Man. In other words: the leader, the hero.

"The Man is the System," 1933.

74.   What machine of government, what system of checks and balances, councils and assemblies, can replace that picture of the Hero turned Father, with a little lamp burning ever beside him as he watches over the labor and the recreation of his people?

Ibid.

75.   Ages can be divided into classical and middle ages: the latter are so characterized because they are in search of unity; the former are those which have found that unity. Classical ages, when complete, can only terminate in one way: consumption, catastrophe, barbarian invasion.

Speech, "Spain and Barbarism," Valladolid, 3-3-35.

76.   But in the midst of the barbarian invasion there have always been saved the larvae of those permanent values that were already contained in the preceding classical age. The barbarians laid low the Roman world, but observe that with their fresh blood they fertilized anew the ideas of the classical world. So also later, the structure of the Middle Ages and the Renaissance was established on spiritual foundations already laid in the ancient world.

Very well: in the Russian Revolution, in the barbarian invasion we are now witnessing, there already lie, concealed and hitherto denied, the gems of a future and better order. It is ours to save those germs and we seek to save them. This is the real task that lies before Spain and our generation: to pass from this last bank of a collapsing economic and social order to the fresh and promising bank of an order that can be descried; but to leap from the one bank to the other by an effort of our will, our impetus and our clairvoyance: to leap from the one bank to the other without being dragged under by the torrent of the barbarian invasion.

Speech, Madrid, 17-11-35.

77.   What is material can be saved by no-one; the thing that matters is that the catastrophe on the material plane shall not wreck the essential values of the spirit too. And these are what we seek to save, cost what it may, even if the price should be the sacrifice of all economic advantages. Their loss is well worth while if Spain, our Spain, shall stem the final invasion of the barbarians.

Speech, "Spain and Barbarism," Valladolid, 3-3-35.

XII.
THEORY OF REVOLUTION

78.   [A] society that knows it has to reform itself is one that is aware of its own injustice, and a society that thinks itself unjust is incapable of defending itself with spirit.

Parliament, 6-11-34.

79.   No one ever risks his life for a material good. Material goods, comparable as they are with one another, are always placed below the higher good which is Life. The time when a man risks a comfortable life, or economic advantages, is when he feels himself filled with a mystic ardor by religion, country, or honor, or by a new sense of the society in which he lives.

Ibid.

80.   Rebellions are always the product of at least two ingredients: the first ingredient, all pervading, is an internal explanation, a want of interior *raison d'être* in the existing regime. This must be present for a rebellion to be raised with any likelihood of success; merely in order that a number of people shall rise in an attempt at rebellion, there must be a certain discontentment, a lack of any vital reason for existence on the part of the regime against which the rebellion is raised. As to this there is no doubt; rebellion have never been raised except against regimes beginning to totter. On the other hand, it is necessary that there shall exist a historical energy which seizes upon this state of discouragement, this want of internal *raison d'être* in the political state it seeks to assail, to launch the attack with more or less good fortune.

Ibid., 25-1-35.

81.   This urge to set everything rolling, come what may, is a frame of mind typical of exhausted and degenerate periods. To set everything rolling is easier than collecting loose ends, tying them up again, sorting

out the serviceable from the perished. . . . Is not perhaps Laziness the Muse of many a revolution?

Tradition and Revolution, August 1935.

82.   The Russian regime in Spain would be hell. But you know from theology that even hell is not absolute evil. In the same way, the Russian regime is not absolute evil either: it is, if you will allow me the expression, hell's version of the urge to a better world.

Speech, Madrid, 17-11-35.

83.   A revolution is always, in principle, something anti-classical. The march of every revolution, however righteous, breaks many harmonious units. But a revolution once set on the move can have but two outcomes: either it swamps everything, or it is canalized. What is impossible is to evade it, to behave as if unaware of its existence.

"F.E.," 7-12-33.

84.   Revolution is needed when, at the end of a long process of decadence, the people has already lost, or is on the point of losing, all historical form.

"Arriba," 30-5-35.

85.   A revolution—if it is to be fruitful and not to be dissipated in ephemeral riots—demands the clear consciousness of a new rule of life and a determined will to apply it.

"Haz," 12-10-35.

86.   Revolution is necessary, not exactly when the people has become corrupted, but when its institutions, ideas and tastes have arrived at sterility or are very near reaching it. At such moments historical degeneration is produced. Not death by cataclysm, but a damming up into puddles without grace and without hope. All collective attitudes are born sickly, as the offspring of a mating of almost exhausted parents. The life of the community grows flat, gets silly, sinks into bad taste and mediocrity. There is no remedy for this except by a clean cut and a fresh start. The furrows need new seed, historic seed, for the old has now come to the end of its fertility. But who is to be the Sower? Who, is to choose the seed and the moment to scatter it over the earth? That is the difficult question.

Ibid.

87.   This truth can escape no-one who meditates over these present moments; at the end of a sterile historical period, when a people—

through its own fault or that of others—has let all the great springs of action go to rust, how is it going to achieve, by itself, the huge task of regeneration . . . ? A sunken people is incapable of discerning and applying the Rule: that very fact is what constitutes its ruin. To have ready to hand the springs that are essential for the accomplishment of a fruitful revolution is an unmistakable sign that revolution is not necessary. And, conversely; to stand in need of revolution is to lack the clearness and drive required to long for it and to carry it through. In a word, peoples *en masse* are incapable of saving themselves, because the fact of being fit to achieve salvation is a proof that one is already safe.

Ibid.

88.   A revolution cannot be achieved by a mass of the people that needs revolution.

Ibid.

89.   Peoples have never been stirred by any but poets; alas for him who, when faced with the poetry of destruction, cannot uplift the poetry of promise!

Speech, Madrid, 29-10-31.

90.   Everyone who throws himself into creating a revolution pledges himself to complete it: what cannot be done is to defraud it.

Parliament, 25-1-35.

91.   [U]nhappy are they who do not come to grips with the roaring torrent of revolution—more or less widespread everywhere today—and turn into useful channels the whole of the impetus it possesses.

"F. E.." 7-12-33.

92.   No revolution produces stable results unless it brings to birth a Caesar of its own. He alone is capable of divining the course of history lying buried beneath the ephemeral clamor of the mass. The masses may not understand him or be grateful to him, but it is he alone who serves them.

"Arriba," 31-10-35.

93.   Revolution is the work of a resolute minority who are proof against discouragement. A minority whose first steps the masses will not understand, because the inner light is the most precious thing they have lost as victims of a decadent period.

"Haz," 12-10-35.

94.   No revolutionary event is or ever has been justified with respect to the preceding juridical order. Every political system that exists in the world, without exception, has been born in open strife with the political order that was in force at the time of its advent; for one of the things not included among the faculties of political orders is the faculty of making a will.

Parliament, 6-6-34.

95.   [A] revolutionary regime is always to be judged by its record, and by its record as viewed in the light of history, not in the light of an episode; its record, which is necessarily assessed by making a comparison between what the revolutionary regime set out to do when it broke with the preceding system, and what it left behind when it concluded its own cycle.

Ibid.

XIII.

COMMAND

96.   Leadership is the supreme office, which exacts every sacrifice, even that of losing all intimacy; which daily demands the divination of things not subject to rules, with the agonizing responsibility of executive action.

Therefore, leadership must be understood with humility, as a post of service, which, come what may, cannot be abandoned out of either impatience, discouragement or cowardice.

"Haz," 12-10-33.

97.   The leader should not obey the public; he should serve it, which is a different thing. To serve it means to direct the exercise of the command for the people's good, achieving the good of the people ruled, even though the people itself be unaware what its good is; in other words, to feel himself in tune with the people's historical destiny, even though dissenting with what the masses feel a desire for.

Ibid.

98.   To be a leader, to be victorious, and to say to the masses next day, "It is you who are in command; I am here to obey you," is a cowardly manner of evading the divine burden of command.

Ibid.

99.   Leaders have no excuse if they desert.

Ibid.

100.   Leaders have no right to any "disenchantment." They cannot capitulate and thus surrender the battered illusions of all those who have followed in their train.

Tribute and Reproach to Ortega, "Haz," 5-12-35.

PART TWO

CRITICISM

PART TWO: CRITICISM

I.

CRITIQUE OF POLITICAL LIBERALISM

101.   Liberalism is, on one hand, the regime without faith, the regime that hands over everything, even the essentials of the country's destiny, to free discussion. For Liberalism, nothing is absolutely true or false. The truth is, in each case, what the greater number of votes say. Thus, it does not matter to Liberalism if a people agrees upon suicide, provided that the proposed suicide is carried out in accordance with electoral practice. . . . And since for the functioning of electoral practice the existence of factions must be encouraged and strife between them must be stimulated, the Liberal system is the system of permanent disunion, permanent want of popular faith in any profound community of destiny.

New Light in Spain, May 1934.

102.   Liberalism brings division, and unrest in the realm of ideas; Socialism opens the even more violent chasm of economic strife in our midst. Under either regime, what becomes of the unity of destiny, without which no people is properly speaking a people at all?

Ibid.

103.   The State believes in nothing; the State believes neither in liberty nor in the sovereignty of the people, for it suspends both whenever required. The State does not even believe itself to be the depository or the executor of a paramount purpose.

Parliament, 6-11-34.

104.   The Liberal State believes in nothing, not even in itself. It stands by with folded arms before experiments of every description, including even those aimed at the destruction of the State itself. It is satisfied if everything develops in accordance with certain regulation forms of procedure. Could anything more foolish be imagined? A State in whose eyes nothing is true elevates to the position of an absolute and unchangeable truth this attitude of doubt, and this alone. It makes a dogma of anti-dogmatism. Hence the Liberals are prepared to let themselves be killed for maintaining that no idea is worth men's while to kill each other for.

1st Open Letter to Luca de Tena, "ABC," 22-3-33.

105.   Liberalism is the mockery of the unfortunate. It proclaims marvelous rights: freedom of thought, freedom to propagate ideas, freedom
of work. . . . But these rights are mere luxuries for the favored ones of
fortune. The poor, in a Liberal regime, may not be bludgeoned into working; but they are starved out. The isolated workman, possessed of every
sort of right on paper, has to choose between dying of starvation and
accepting the terms the capitalist offers him, however hard they may be.
Under the Liberal system the cruel irony could be seen of men and
women working themselves to skeletons, twelve hours a day, for a mis-
erable wage, and yet being assured by the law that they were "free" men
and women.

New Light in Spain, May 1934.

106.   When in March 1762 a man of ill omen called Jean Jacques
Rousseau published *The Social Contract*, political truth ceased to be a
permanent entity. Previously, in ages that were more profound, States,
which were the executors of historic missions, had inscribed upon their
brows, and even upon the stars, the words Justice and Truth. Jean Jacques
Rousseau came to tell us that justice and truth were not permanent categories of reason, but that they were, at any given moment, decisions of
the will.

Speech, Madrid, 29-10-33.

107.   The Geneva philosopher is a sickly man, delicate and refined;
he is a philosopher who, as Spengler tells us happens to all Romantics—
and this man was by now a direct precursor of Romanticism—was fa-
tigued by the feel of living in too healthy, too virile and too robust a
society. He was crushed by the weight of such a fully adult society, and
felt as it were constrained to leave it, to return to nature, to free himself
from discipline, harmony, and rule.

This yearning for Nature is the keynote of all his writings: the return
to freedom. The most famous of his books whose influence was to last
throughout the nineteenth century and only began to lose its grip in practically our own times, does not, as you have so often read, begin absolutely, but it almost does, with a sentence which is a sigh. It reads: "Man
is born free, and finds himself everywhere in fetters." This philosopher,
as you are all aware, was called Jean Jacques Rousseau; the book was
called *The Social Contract*.

The Social Contract seeks to deny the justification of those authorities received traditionally by reason of either a supposedly divine ap-
pointment or one based upon the tradition. He seeks to deny the justification of these powers and to begin the building afresh on the basis of
his own nostalgia for freedom. He says: "Man is free: man is free by

nature and cannot in any way divest himself of being free. There cannot be any system but that which he accepts of his own free will; his freedom he can never renounce, because it would be equivalent to renouncing his quality of being human. Moreover, if he were to renounce freedom, he would be entering into an agreement void for want of value received in exchange; he cannot but be free and unrenounceably free. Consequently, no form of State can possibly arise in opposition to the free wills of those that make up a society; the origin of political societies must have been Contract. This contract, the aggregate of these wills, engenders a higher Will, a will which is not the sum, total of the others, but self-subsistent. It is a different ego, superior and indifferent to the personalities that produced it by their presence. Very well: this sovereign will, this will now detached from the other wills, is the only one that may legislate: this is the only one that may impose itself on men without men's having any claim against it, because if they turned against it, they would be turning against themselves. This sovereign will can neither err nor seek the evil of its subjects.

Lecture, Madrid, 9-4-35.

108.   Jean Jacques Rousseau supposed that the agglomeration of all of us who live as a nation possesses a higher soul, one belonging to a hierarchy different from that of each of our own souls, and that this higher ego is endowed with an infallible will, able at any instant to define justice and injustice, good and evil. And as this collective will, this sovereign will, is expressed by means of suffrage alone—a majority conjecture that triumphs over the minority one in the matter of divining what the higher will may be—the eventual result was that suffrage, that farce of little paper slips going into a glass ballot-box, possessed the power of telling us at any moment if God existed or not, if, the truth was true or untrue, and if our country ought to continue or if on the other hand it was better that it should commit suicide.

Speech, Madrid, 29-10-33.

109.   The Revolution finds the principles of Rousseau already developed, and adopts them. In the Constitution of 1789, in that of '91, in that of '93, in that of the third year, in that of the eighth year, the principle of national sovereignty is formulated almost in the same words used by Rousseau: "The principle of all sovereignty resides essentially in the nation. No corporation and no individual can exercise authority which does not emanate expressly therefrom." Do not imagine that the mere declaration of this gives rise to universal suffrage at the same time. It is only in one of the French revolutionary constitutions, that of 1793, that this principle got applied and this suffrage established. In the rest it did not;

in the rest, suffrage is restricted, and in that of the eighth year it even disappears; but the principle is always formulated in the words: "All sovereignty resides essentially in the Nation." Nevertheless, there is something in the revolutionary Constitutions that was not in the Social Contract, and this is the declaration of the Rights of Man. I said just now that Rousseau did not allow the individual to reserve to himself anything as against that sovereign will, that sovereign ego constituted by the national will. Rousseau did not allow this; the revolutionary Constitutions did. But it was Rousseau who was right. The time was to come when the power of the Assemblies became so great that in reality the power of the single man disappeared, and it was illusory for any kind of rights that the individual had reserved to himself to seek to prevail against that power.

Lecture, Madrid, 9-4-35.

110.   As the Liberal State was a faithful servant of this doctrine, it gradually constituted itself as no longer the resolute executor of the country's destinies but as a spectator of electoral struggles. For the Liberal State the only important thing was that there should be, seated at the voting tables, a certain number of gentlemen; that the elections should begin at eight o'clock and end at four; and that the ballot-boxes should not be broken. Whereas being broken is the noblest destiny of any ballot-box. Thereafter, to observe with calm respect what should issue forth from the ballot-boxes, as if it had itself no interest therein. In other words, the Liberal rulers did not even believe in their own mission; they did not believe that they themselves were there to fulfil a duty worthy of respect, but that anyone who thought the contrary and set about assailing the State, by fair means or foul, had just as good a right to say so and to do so as the guardians of the State itself had to defend it. Hence arose the democratic system, which is, in the first place, the most ruinous possible system for the squandering of energy. A man endowed with gifts for the high function of governing, which is perhaps the noblest of all human functions, was obliged to devote 80, 90, or 95 percent of his energies to making good the routine objections of opposition, to the making of election propaganda, to sleeping whole nights on parliamentary benches, to flattering electors, to enduring their impertinencies, because it was from the hands of the electors that he was going to get power; to tolerating humiliation and indignities at the hands of those who, by very reason of the quasi-divine function of governing, were required to obey him; and then, after all this, if he had a few hours left towards daybreak or a few moments stolen from an uneasy repose, it was in this minute period to spare that the man endowed with gifts for governing was able to give serious thought to the substantive functions of Government.

Later, there came the loss of the spiritual unity of peoples, for as the system worked by achievement of majorities, every object that the system set itself to gain had to obtain a majority of the votes. And it had to obtain them by stealing them, if necessary, from the other parties; and for this reason it had to have no hesitation in calumniating them, in heaping upon them the vilest obloquies, in deliberately falsifying the truth, in not letting slip a single means of lying and vilification. And thus, fraternity being one of the postulates displayed before our eyes on the title page of the Liberal State, there has never been a collective condition of life in which wronged men, at enmity one with another, have ever felt themselves less fraternal than in the turbulent and unpleasant life of the Liberal State.

Finally, the Liberal State came to involve us in economic slavery, for the workers were told, with tragic sarcasm: "You are free to work as you wish; no-one can compel you to accept these conditions or those; very well then, as we are the rich, we offer you the conditions we think fit; you, as free citizens, are not obliged to accept them if you do not want to; but you, as poor citizens, if you do not accept the conditions that we impose upon you, will die of starvation, surrounded by the greatest degree of Liberal dignity."

                                                    Speech, Madrid, 29-10-33.

111.   Liberalism (it may be described thus because the raising of a barrier against tyranny was just what the revolutionary Constitutions aimed at), liberalism has its great period, the one during which it establishes all men as equals before the law, a victory from which there can now be no retrocession. But this victory once achieved, and its great period over, liberalism begins to find itself with nothing to do, and spends its time destroying itself. Naturally enough, what Rousseau termed the sovereign will becomes reduced to the will of the majority. According to Rousseau, it was the majority—theoretically, through its faculty of divining and expressing the sovereign will, but in practice through its triumph over the dissident minority—which should prevail over all; the achievement of this majority implied that the parties had to enter into conflict so as to win more votes than their rivals; that they had to make propaganda against one another, after first having broken up themselves. In other words, it is precisely under the thesis of supposedly indivisible national sovereignty that opinions are most divided, for as each group seeks that its own will shall be identified with the presumptive sovereign will, the groups grow more and more obliged to define themselves, to adopt distinctive attitudes, to fight, to destroy one another, and to try to win the electoral battles. Thus it comes about that in the decomposition of the liberal system (of course, this transit or march-past, which has been

summed up in a few minutes, is a process lasting many years), in this decomposition of the liberal system, the parties become so broken up that when the regime has reached its last gasp in some parts of Europe, as it did in the Germany of the days just before Hitler, there were no less than thirty-two parties. In Spain, I should not dare to state what they all are, because I myself do not know; indeed, I do not even know the ones represented in Parliament, for apart from all the groups officially represented and those fused into parliamentary blocs, and apart from the Members who, either alone or with one or two bosom friends, parade under a group denomination, there is in our Parliament—as Don Mariano Matesanz is aware—one extraordinarily odd thing: two minorities, each composed of ten gentlemen, and calling themselves Independent Minorities; but, mark you, not because as being minorities they are independent of the rest, but because each one of their component individuals regards himself as being independent of all the others.

So that those who belong to these minorities—to which neither Don Mariano Matesanz nor I belong, since we are independent altogether; those who belong to these minorities owe their grouping together and their connecting-link to just their characteristic note of not being in agreement. In other words, the only thing they agree about is that they don't agree about anything. And, naturally, apart from this pulverisation of parties, or rather, on emerging from this pulverisation of parties through the conditional union of one or two parties, we then observe the phenomenon that the majority—half Parliament plus one Member or half Parliament plus two—feels invested with the full sovereign power of the nation to exploit or crush the rest, not merely of the Members but of the Spanish people; it feels itself to be the holder of a limitless power of self-justification, in other words it feels itself endowed with authority to carry through whatever it thinks fit, without paying any further attention to any kind of personal judgment, juridical or human, so far as the rest of mankind is concerned.

Jean Jacques Rousseau had foreseen something of this kind, when he said: "Very good; but as the sovereign will is indivisible and moreover incapable of error, if by chance a man even finds himself in conflict with the sovereign will, it is the man who is in error; and at such a time, when the sovereign will constrains him to submit to it, it is doing nothing but compelling him to be free." Observe the sophistry, and just consider whether, for instance, when we Members of the Republican Parliament, undeniably the representatives of the national sovereignty, increase your taxes or invent some other uncomfortable law to annoy you with, it has ever occurred to you to think that in this act of raising your taxes or annoying you a little more, we have been carrying out the benevolent task of making you a little more free, whether you liked it nor not.

Lecture, Madrid, 9-4-35.

II.

CRITIQUE OF ECONOMIC LIBERALISM

112.   Property, in the sense that we have been hitherto regarding it, is coming to its end. The masses, who to a great extent are right, and who moreover have the power, are going to put paid to it, by peaceful means or by violence.

Speech, "Spain and Barbarism," Valladolid, 3-3-35.

113.   Capital . . . is an economic instrument which must serve the entire economy, and hence may not be an instrument for the advantage and privilege of the few who have had the good luck to get in first.

Lecture, Madrid, 9-4-35.

114.   Property is not capital: capital is an economic tool, and as a tool it must be put to the service of the economic whole, not the personal wellbeing of any one person. The reservoirs of capital should be like the reservoirs of water; not constructed so that one or two people may hold regattas on the surface, but so that the flow of rivers may be regulated and the hydro-electric plants may be driven.

Speech, "Spain and Barbarism," Valladolid, 3-3-35.

115.   On the other hand, we have the Scots economist. The Scots economist is another type of man: he is a formal, precise man, simple in his tastes, somewhat Voltairian, rather abstracted and somewhat melancholy. This economist, before he was one, expounded Logic in Glasgow University, and, later, Moral Philosophy. At that time Moral Philosophy was composed of several quite different things: Natural Theology, Ethics, Jurisprudence and Politics. He had even written a book in the year 1759, a book entitled *Theory of Moral Feeling*; but, in reality, it is not this book that opened the gates of immortality to him; the book that opened the gates of immortality to him is entitled *Investigations Concerning the Wealth of Nations*. The Scots economist, as you have all guessed by now, was called Adam Smith.

Very well: for Adam Smith, the economic world was a natural community created by the division of labor. This division of labor was not a conscious phenomenon, sought by those who had split up the tasks among themselves; it was an unconscious phenomenon, a spontaneous phenomenon. Men had been going on splitting up the work without any common understanding; no-one, in proceeding to make this division, had been guided by the interest of the rest, but merely by utility to himself. Which comes to this, that each one, in seeking this utility to himself, had arrived at harmony with the utility of the rest, and so, in this spontaneous, free society, there appear: first, labor, which is the sole source of wealth; next, barter, that is to say the exchange of the things we produce ourselves for the things produced by others; then, money, which is a merchandise that everyone is certain will be accepted by the rest; finally, capital, which is the saving of that which we have not had to spend, the saving of produced wealth in order to be able with it to give life to fresh enterprises. Adam Smith believed that capital was the indispensable condition of industry: capital makes industry possible, to use his own words. But all this happens automatically, as I say: no-one has made any agreement for this to work thus, and nevertheless it works thus and it must word thus. Moreover Adam Smith considers that it ought to work thus, and he is so sure and so pleased with this proof he has been stringing together, that he turns to the State, the Sovereign—he also calls it the sovereign—and he says: "The best thing that you can do is not to interfere with anything. Let things be as they are. The things of economy are very delicate; don't touch them, and if you don't touch them, they'll work by themselves and work well."

Lecture, Madrid, 9-4-35.

116.   In the same way as Rousseau found that the French Revolution a little later adopted his principles, so Adam Smith had the luck, rarely attained by any writer, of having England also adopt his economic principles. She opened her doors to the free play of supply and demand, which, according, to Adam Smith, would, without more ado or exertion by anyone else, produce economic equilibrium. And, in fact, economic liberalism too had its heroic age of life, a magnificently heroic age. We must never vilify the fallen, either the physically fallen, the men, who as men, even if they were our enemies merit all the respect due to their human quality and dignity, or the ideologically fallen. Economic liberalism did have a great period, a magnificent period of splendor; to its drive and initiative was due the enormous expansion in production of hitherto unexploited wealth, the accessibility, even to the lowest income groups, of great inventions and conveniences; while competition and abundance undeniably raised the standard of living of many. Well now, what was going to bring economic liberalism to its death was the fact that very soon it was to give birth, as its own child, to that tremendous phenomenon, perhaps the most tremendous of our epoch, which is known as capitalism; and from now on I think we are no longer relating ancient history.

I should like us once and for all to be clear with ourselves on the matter of words. When we speak of capitalism, we are not referring to private property; the two things are not only different, but one might almost describe them as opposed; one of the effects of capitalism was just the annihilation, almost entirely, of private property in its traditional forms. This is reasonably clear in everyone's mind, but it may not be superfluous for me to devote a few words of further explanation to the subject. Capitalism is the transformation, more or less rapidly, of what is the direct link between a man and his goods, into an instrument of power. The property of former times, the property of the craftsman, of the small producer, of the small trader, is as it were a projection of the individual upon his goods. He is their proprietor in so far as he is able to have these goods, use them, enjoy them, exchange them; if you like, it is practically in those words that the conception of property has resided, for centuries, in Roman law. But in proportion as capitalism grows more perfect and complicated, you will observe how the relationship between a man and his goods becomes more distant, and how a series of technical instruments of domination begins to come between them. What was the direct, human, elementary projection of relationship between a man and his goods gets more involved: symbols begin to be introduced which cover the representation of a property-relationship, but they are symbols that more and more tend to replace the living presence of the man; and when capitalism reaches its final stage of perfection, the real proprietor of the former property is no longer a man, nor a group of men, but an abstraction represented by slips of paper; this is the case in what is called the anonymous company. The anonymous company is the real proprietor of a whole heap of legal rights, and up to such a point has it dehumanized itself, to such a pitch is it indifferent to the human proprietor of those rights, that the exchange of shares by their holders has no effect whatsoever upon the juridical organization or the functioning of the company as a whole.

Thus, this great capital, this technical capital, this capital which attains huge proportions, not only has nothing to do, as I said, with property in the elementary human sense of the word, but is hostile to it. That is why on many occasions, when I see how employers and workmen, for instance, reach the stage of violent conflict, even to the point of killing one another in the streets, even to the point of falling victims to outrages that express a savage hatred past all repair, I think to myself that neither side is aware that they are protagonists in an economic struggle, certainly, but one in which nine times out of ten both lots of them are on the same side. The other side, opposed to both employers and workmen, is the power of capitalism, the technique of finance-capitalism. If this is not true, then tell me, you who have far more experience than I have in such things: how often have you had to go to the great credit houses to ask for economic aid, well aware that they charge you interest at the rate of 7 or 8 percent, and equally well aware that this money they lend you does not belong to the institution that is lending it, but belongs to those who have deposited it and who are receiving 1, 5, or 2 percent interest themselves? This huge difference that they charge you for passing the money from one hand to another weighs jointly upon you and your workmen, who maybe are even now waiting round a corner to kill you.

It is this finance-capital, then, which has been travelling towards its own collapse in recent decades. Note that its collapse takes place in two ways: first, from the social point of view (as indeed was almost to be expected), and secondly, from the point of view of capitalist technique itself, as we are shortly about to show.

From the social point of view, you will see that I am going to find myself quite involuntarily in agreement on more than one point with the criticism made by Karl Marx. As in fact all of us, now that we have flung ourselves into politics, have to speak of him constantly as we have all of us had to declare ourselves Marxists or anti-Marxists. Karl Marx appears to some people—naturally not to any of you—as a sort of Utopia-spinner. We have even seen in print the expression "the Utopian dreams of Karl Marx." You are only too well aware that if there has been one man in the world who was not a dreamer, that man was Karl Marx. The one thing his implacable spirit did was to plant himself down before the living reality of the British economic organization of the Manchester factories, and deduce that within that economic structure there were at work a number of constant factors which would end by destroying it. This is what Karl Marx said in a book of appalling bulk, which he was not able to complete within his lifetime, but a book, to tell the truth, as interesting as it is bulky; a book of the most closely-reasoned dialectic and of extraordinary ingenuity; a book, as I say, of pure criticism, in which, after prophesying that the society based on this system would end by destroying itself, he did not even take the trouble to say when or in what form its destruction was to come upon it. He did no more than say: given such and such premises, I deduce that this is going to end badly; and then he died, even before publishing volumes two and three of his work, and he went to the other world (I dare not say to hell as that would be a rash judgment), without the slightest suspicion of the fact that one day a Spanish anti-Marxist was to arise who would range him among the poets.

This Karl Marx long since augured the social collapse of capitalism which I am discussing with you now. He saw that the following things at least were going to occur: first, the accumulation of capital, which cannot fail to be produced by large-scale industry. Small-scale industry worked with practically two ingredients alone: labor and raw material.

In periods of crisis, these two things were easy to reduce: less raw material was bought, the number of hands employed was reduced, and production was roughly equated to the market's demands. But large-scale industry comes into being, and large-scale industry, apart from that element which Marx himself calls variable capital, employs a vast part of its reserves in fixed capital—a vast part, far exceeding the value of the raw materials and wages of labor; and it sets up great installations of machinery which cannot be instantaneously reduced. Hence, if production is to repay this vast concentration of dead capital, there is nothing this type of industry can do but produce on an enormous scale, as it does; and as it produces cheaper by dint of increasing the volume of production, it invades the small producer's domain, ruining them one by one, and ends by absorbing them all.

This law of accumulation of capital was predicted by Marx, and although some say it has not been fulfilled, we are beginning to see that it has, for Europe and the world are full of trusts, huge producers federations and other things that you know more about than I do, like these magnificent one-price stores, which can allow themselves the luxury of selling at dumping rates as they know you cannot stand more than a few months competition with them, whereas they, on the contrary, by balancing some establishments against others and some branches against others, can fold their arms and await your complete annihilation.

The second phenomenon that supervenes is proletarianization. Craftsmen displaced from their positions, craftsmen who have been the owners of their own means of production and who naturally have had to sell this as it is now useless to them, as also small manufacturers and small traders, continue to get economically crushed by this huge, colossal, irresistible advance of big capital, and end by becoming incorporated in the proletaries, and proletarianized. Marx describes this in remarkably dramatic terms and he says that these men, after selling their products, selling the means they had of manufacturing their products, and selling their houses, have now nothing left to sell, and they then realize that they themselves can be a form of merchandise, their very labor can be a form of merchandise, and they rush to the market to hire themselves out in temporary slavery. This phenomenon, then, the proletarianization of vast masses, and their conglomeration round city factories, is another symptom of the social bankruptcy of capitalism.

Yet there is still another to be produced, and that is unemployment. In the first days of the introduction of machinery, the workmen resisted its introduction into the workshops. They reckoned that these machines, which could do the work of twenty, a hundred, or four hundred workmen, were going to displace them. As those were the days of faith in "indefinite progress," the economist of the day said with a smile: "These ignorant working men do not realize that what this is going to do is to increase production, develop trade, provide a greater volume of business; there will be room for machines and for men." But it proved that there was not, for in many parts machines have displaced almost the whole of the men, to the most exorbitant degree. For example, in the Czechoslovakian bottle-production—these data occur to my mind—in which 8,000 workmen were employed, not in 1880 but in 1920, there are at this moment only 1,000 employed, and the production of bottles has nevertheless increased.

The displacement of men by machines is not accompanied by even the poetical compensation attributed to the machine in former times, that compensation which consisted in relieving men of the heavy burden of labor. It was said: "No the machines will do our work, the machines will free us from our toil." This poetical compensation does not exist, for what the machines have done has not been to reduce the men's working day, but, while maintaining the working day more or less unchanged—for the reduction in working hours is due to different causes—to displace all the surplus men. Nor has it had the compensation of involving an increase in wages. It is clear that workmen's wages have increased; but here again we must repeat everything truthfully just as we find it in the statistics. In the prosperity period in the United States, from 1922 to 1929, do you know how much the total volume of wages paid to workmen went up? Well, it went up 5 percent. And do you know how much dividends on capital went up during the same period? Well, it was 86 percent. Tell me if that is a fair way of sharing the advantages of mechanization!

But it was predictable that capitalism should have this social collapse. What was less predictable was that it should also have a technical collapse, which is perhaps what is bringing its position to such desperate straits.

For instance: periodic crises have been a phenomenon produced by large-scale industry and produced by exactly the same cause I mentioned before, when I dealt with the accumulation of capital. The irrecoverable expenditure of the original installation is dead-weight expenditure which can in no case be reduced as the market shrinks. Overproduction, the overproduction on a violent scale of which I spoke before, ends by saturating the markets. Then under-consumption is produced, and the market absorbs less than the factories are delivering to it. If the structure of the former small-scale economic system had been preserved, production would decline in proportion to demand by means of a diminution in the intake of raw materials and labor; but as this cannot be done in the case of large-scale industry, since it has this vast fixed capital, large-scale industry is ruined; that is to say, technically large-scale industry has to face periods of worse crisis than small. This is the first collapse of its erstwhile pride.

Afterwards, however, one of the most pleasing and attractive notes of the heroic age of liberal capitalism fails also: that pride of its earliest days, which said: "I have no need whatsoever of public assistance, nay, I request the public authorities to leave me in peace and not to interfere in my affairs." In a very short space of time capitalism bows its head in this domain also, and as soon as the periods of crisis arrive it has recourse to public assistance, and so we have seen how the most powerful concerns have resorted to the benevolence of the State, either to gain tariff protection or to obtain financial support. In other words, to quote a writer hostile to the capitalist system, the capitalism which is so haughty and so refractory in the matter of a possible socialization of its profits, is the first to beg, when things are going badly, for the socialization of its losses.

Finally, another advantage of free exchange and liberal economics consisted in the stimulation of competition. It was said—"By competing in an open market, all producers will be continually perfecting their products, and the position of those who buy them will get better and better." But large-scale capitalism has automatically eliminated competition by placing all production in the hands of a few powerful concerns.

Thus have come about all the results we have seen: crisis, proletarianization, paralysis, closing of factories, the huge array of proletarians without employment, the European war, the post-war days—and man, who aspired to live within a liberal economic and political system and under liberal principles that filled such a political and economic life with substance and hope, came in the end to find himself reduced to this appalling state. Formerly he was a craftsman or a small manufacturer, perhaps a member of some privileged corporation, or a citizen of a powerful Municipality. Today he is none of these.

Man has been gradually stripped of all his attributes, he has been left chemically pure in his condition of individual; he has nothing now, he has only day and night; he has not even a piece of land of his own to set his foot on, or a house to lodge in; the citizenship of old, complete, human, integral, and full, has been reduced to these two pitiable things: a number on the electoral roll and a number in the queue at the factory gates. And then look at the double prospect for Europe: on the one hand, a nearness of the possibility of war: Europe, despairing, out of gear, nerve-racked, may well rush into another war. And on the other hand, the attraction of Russia, the attraction of Asia, for you should not forget the Asiatic ingredient in what is called Russian Communism, in which there is as much or more influence typically anarchistic and Asiatic as there is of Germanic Marxian influence. Lenin proclaimed, as the last stage in the regime he sought to implant—he proclaimed it in the book he published shortly before the triumph of the Russian revolution—that in the end there would come about a Stateless and classless society. This last stage had all the characteristics of the anarchism of Bakunin and Kropotkin; but to reach this stage it was necessary to pass through another most grievous and Marxian one, the dictatorship of the proletariat, and Lenin, with extraordinarily cynical irony, observed: "This stage will not be free or just. The State's mission is to oppress; all States oppress; the working-class State too will have to be an oppressor. What occurs is that it will be oppressing the recently expropriated class, the class that hitherto oppressed it. The State will not be free or just. And, moreover, the transition to the final stage, that venturesome stage of communist anarchism, will come we know not when." That time is one that it has not yet reached yet; probably it never will reach it. To a European consciousness, to the consciousness of a European bourgeoisie or proletarians, this is a matter for dread and for despair. True, what they have reached in that country is dissolution in multiplicity of number, and oppression beneath the iron heel of the State. But the despairing European proletarians, which can find no explanation for its own existence in Europe, looks on the Russian thing as a myth, as a remote possibility of liberation.

Ibid.

117.   Note how far the final decay of political and economic liberalism has brought us: it has presented huge European masses with this frightful dilemma: either a fresh war, which will be the suicide of Europe, or else Communism, which will mean handing Europe over to Asia.

Ibid.

III.
CRITIQUE OF MARXISM

118.   Liberalism, while writing marvelous Declarations of Rights on a piece of paper which practically nobody read—among other reasons, because the people were not even taught to read; while Liberalism was writing these declarations, it was making us spectators of the most inhuman sight ever witnessed—in the greatest cities of Europe, in capitals of States with the finest liberal institutions, human beings, brothers of ours, were being huddled together in formless, horrifying black or red houses, shackled by want and by the tuberculosis and anemia of hungry children,

and enduring every so often the sarcasm of being told that they were free and sovereign to boot.

Speech, Valladolid, 4-3-34.

119.   Can a cruder form of existence be conceived than that of the proletarians, living perhaps for twenty years by making the same screw in the same immense factory-nave, without ever seeing the complete assembly of which that screw forms part, and with no other link to bind them to the factory than the inhuman frigidity of the payroll?

Tradition and Revolution, August 1935.

120.   The whole of this spectacle of the crisis of capitalism which we are witnessing was prophesied by one figure—in part a grim, in part a fascinating one—the figure of Karl Marx. Today everybody round here, talks about being Marxist or anti-Marxist. Now I am asking you, in the same strict sense, like an examination of conscience, that I am putting into my own words: What is the meaning of being an anti-Marxist? Does it mean not desiring the fulfilment of Marx's predictions? In that case, we are all in agreement. Or does it mean that Marx was mistaken in his predictions? In that case the mistake is committed by those who impute the error to him.

Speech, Madrid, 19-5-35.

121.   For this reason, Socialism was bound to be born, and its birth was justified (we are not people who shrink from any truth). The working men had to defend themselves against that system, which gave them promises of rights, but was not at any pains to provide them with a decent life. But today Socialism, which was a legitimate reaction against that Liberal enslavement, has gone astray, because it has adopted, first, the materialist interpretation of life and history; secondly, an attitude of revenge; thirdly, the enunciation of the class-struggle dogma.

Socialism, above all the socialism constructed in the passionless frigidity of their drawing-rooms by the Socialist apostles in whom the poor working men believed, and who have been displayed to our eyes for what they really were by Alfonso García Valdecasas; Socialism, thus understood, sees nothing in history but the play of economic forces; everything spiritual is suppressed, religion is the opium of the people, patriotism is a myth for the exploitation of the under-dog; Socialism says all this. Nothing exists but production and economic organization. Workmen, therefore, must wring their souls well out, lest the least drop of spirituality should remain within them.

Socialism does not aspire to re-establish a social justice that has broken down through the faulty functioning of the Liberal State; rather, it aims at reprisal. It aspires to attain a point so many degrees higher in injustice, the higher the injustice of the Liberal system has risen.

Finally, Socialism proclaims the monstrous dogma of class warfare; it proclaims the dogma that warfare between classes is indispensable and is produced naturally in life, because there is no possibility of there ever being any appeasing agent. So Socialism, which started out as a just critique of economic liberalism, has brought us, by a different route, the same fruits as economic liberalism: disunity, hatred, separation, forgetfulness of every bond of brotherhood and solidarity between men.

Speech, Madrid, 29-10-33.

122.   The class struggle had a just motive, and Socialism at the beginning was in the right; there is no purpose in denying this. What has happened is that instead of pursuing its original path of seeking after social justice among men, Socialism has turned into a mere doctrine, and one of the chilliest frigidity, and it has no concern, great or small, for the liberation of working men. There are working men going about here full of pride in themselves and calling themselves Marxists. Many streets in many Spanish towns have now been dedicated to Karl Marx; but Karl Marx was a German Jew who sat in his study and watched, with horrible impassivity, the most dramatic happenings of his age. He was a German Jew who, with the British factories in Manchester before his eyes, and in the middle of formulating inexorable laws about the accumulation of capital, in the middle of formulating inexorable laws about production and about the interests of employers and workmen, was all the time writing letters to his friend Friedrich Engels, telling him the workers were a mob and a rabble, which need not be bothered with except in so far as they might serve to test out his doctrines.

Socialism stopped being a movement for the redemption of men, and came to be, as I say, a remorseless doctrine, and instead of seeking to reestablish a system of justice, sought to achieve injustice,—by way of reprisal, to the same extent as bourgeois injustice had reached in its own system of organization. In addition, however, it set up the class struggle as something that would never cease, and it further declared that history is to be interpreted materialistically; in other words, that for the explanation of history none but economic phenomena count. Thus, when Marxism culminates in an organization such as the Russian, children in schools are told that Religion is the opium of the people, that "Patria" is a word invented for purposes of oppression, and that even chastity and the love of parents for their children are bourgeois prejudices to be extirpated at all costs.

This is what Socialism has come to mean. Do you think that if working people knew this they would feel attracted by anything like this terrifying, horrible, inhuman thing conceived by the brain of that Jew who called himself Karl Marx?

Speech, Valladolid, 4-3-34.

123.   On dehumanizing itself in the inhospitable mind of Marx, Socialism turned into a crude and frigid doctrine of strife. Since that day it has not aimed at social justice; it aims at paying off an old score of hate, by imposing upon the tyrants of yesterday—the bourgeoisie—a dictatorship of the proletariat.

New Light in Spain, May 1934.

124.   Marx's prophecies are being fulfilled faster or slower, but inexorably. We are moving towards the concentration of capital; we are moving towards the proletarianization of the masses; and we are moving, last of all, towards the social revolution, which will have a very severe period of Communist dictatorship. And it is this Communist dictatorship that we are bound to shrink from in horror as Europeans, Westerners, and Christians, for this indeed is an appalling negation of man; this is indeed the absorption of man into a vast amorphous mass, in which all individuality is lost and the corporeal vesture of each individual immortal soul is weakened and dissolved. Note well that this is why we are anti-Marxists: we are anti-Marxists because it horrifies us, as it horrifies every Westerner, whether employer or proletarian, this being like some creature of the lower animal life in an ant heap. And it horrifies us because we know something of it from capitalism; capitalism too is international and materialistic. That is why we want neither the one nor the other; that is why we want to avoid the fulfilment of Karl Marx's predictions—because we believe his assertions. But what we want we want resolutely; not like those anti-Marxist parties walking about the place who think that the inexorable fulfilment of economic and historical laws can be whittled down by saying a few kind words to the workers and sending them little knitted jackets for their children.

Speech, Madrid, 19-5-35.

125.   If the Socialist revolution were nothing more than the setting up of a new order in the economic field, we should not be alarmed. The fact is that the Socialist revolution is something far deeper. It is the victory of the materialist interpretation of life and history; it is the violent substitution of irreligion for religion; the substitution of the closed and embittered Class for the Patria; the grouping of men by classes and not the grouping of men of all classes within the Patria which is common to them

all; it is the replacement of individual freedom by an iron subjection to a State which not only regulates our labor, as in an ant heap, but also implacably regulates our recreation. It is all that. It is the sweeping advent of an order that annihilates western Christian civilization; it is the sign that marks the close of a civilization which we, brought up as we are in its essential values, decline to recognize as doomed.

Speech, Madrid, 2-2-36.

126.   Yesterday morning I was definitely described as a Bolshevik. . . . What conception of the Bolsheviks can my detractors have formed? Do they think that Bolshevism consists, above everything else, in cutting up landed estates and putting back upon them a people that has starved for centuries? If so, they are mistaken. Bolshevism is at heart a materialistic attitude towards the world. Bolshevism may be able to resign itself to failure in its attempts at collectivized farming, but it will never make concessions in that which is of paramount importance: the uprooting of all religion from the people, the destruction of the family cell, the materialization of existence. He who starts from a merely economic interpretation of history is on the way towards Bolshevism. Hence anti-Bolshevism is exactly the position of those who regard the world beneath the sign of spiritual things. These two attitudes, not calling themselves Bolshevism or anti-Bolshevism, have always been in existence. Bolshevik, everyone who aims at winning material advantages for himself and his own set, come what may. Anti-Bolshevik, he who is prepared to go without material enjoyments in order to maintain spiritual values. The old nobles who pledged life and property to the service of Religion, King, and Country, were the negation of Bolshevism. Those of us today who, in face of a wheezing capitalist system, sacrifice comforts and profits in order to bring about a reformation of the world without smashing the things of the spirit, are the negation of Bolshevism. It may be that our less vituperated labors will succeed in consolidating some centuries of life that will be less luxurious for the elect but will not be passed beneath the sign of savagery and blasphemy. On the other hand, those who anchor themselves to the endless enjoyment of unearned wealth, those who deem it more important and more urgent to satisfy their uttermost wish for superfluities than to relieve the hunger of a whole people—they, the materialistic—interpreters of the world, are the real

Bolsheviks. And it is a Bolshevism with a horrible refinement added: the Bolshevism of the privileged.

Remarks by a Bolshevik, "ABC," 31-7-35.

IV.
SPANISH LIBERALISM

127.   It might be said that Liberalism, outside Spain, had never been more than an "Intellectual," a sort of joke during times of ease. France, for example, who did most to put Liberalism into circulation, takes good care to stow it in the cellar when things begin to look serious. In France one does not play tricks with the police (established by Napoleon), or with the law (with the guillotine and Devil's Island at its disposal), or with the Patria (furnished with inexorable Courts-Martial). Liberalism provides a subject of conversation, and the toleration of superficial license.

"Libertad," Valladolid, 22-10-34.

128.   In actual fact, our political liberalism and our economic liberalism have been almost spared the trouble of decaying, because they have barely at any time existed. You already know what political liberalism meant. Elections, until quite recent times, were arranged in the Ministry for Home Affairs, and there were even a large number of Spaniards who congratulated themselves that this was so. One of the most brilliant of Spaniards, Angel Ganivet, back in the year 1887, said more or less this: "Fortunately, we have in Spain one admirable institution, namely the *encasillado* system[5]." This avoids the holding of elections, for on the day when elections are held, the results will be very serious. Obviously, in order to gain the support of the masses, very crude and easily comprehended ideas must be put into circulation, because difficult ideas cannot be brought home to multitudes and as it will then be the case that the best gifted men will not feel very eager to walk about the streets shaking hands with the worthy electors and talking fatuities to them, it will end up in the triumph of those from whom fatuities proceed as a natural and typical characteristic. Some years later—I think it was in 1893—recalcitrant and tenacious as ever of his anti-democratic attitude, he reached the point of saying: "I am an enthusiastic admirer of universal suffrage, on one condition—that nobody votes." And he added; "Let it not be thought that this is merely a joke in bad taste. I realize that in essence, in principle, all men should take part in their country's affairs of state, just as I find the perfect position for man is to be a paterfamilias; but as the two things are so difficult, I advise all the men I see on the way to contracting marriage not to do so, and those I find prepared for voting, I advise not

---

[5] *Encasillado* system: "Lists of candidates affiliated to the Government and allotted electoral constituencies by the latter." Casares's Ideological Dictionary.

to vote. Fortunately, the Spanish people has no need of this counsel because it has itself decided not to vote."

Such, indeed, has been our political liberalism. And when it stopped
being like that, and there were real elections, we have witnessed the sight
of a Parliament which, convinced that electoral victory empowered it to
do whatever it saw fit, did so indeed, even up to the point of crushing the
rest of humanity.

But apart from this fluctuation between the liberal regime which had
no existence and the Parliament which had too much, we discover that
the Spanish State, the Spanish Constitutional State, as we see it deline-
ated in its fundamental charter and ancillary statutes, does not exist; it is
a mere joke, a mere simulacrum of existence. The Spanish State does not
exist in any one of its most important institutions.

Lecture, Madrid, 9-4-35.

129.   Spanish capitalism was rickety from the start; from its begin-
nings it started limping along supported by State aid and tariff assistance.
Our economy was more impoverished than almost any other countries'
and our people lived in greater want than almost any other.

Speech, Madrid, 19-5-35.

130.   Neither did economic liberalism, in reality, require to fail in
Spain, because the best period of economic liberalism, the heroic age of
capitalism in its original stages, was never experienced, generally speaking, by Spanish capital at all. Here big business had recourse to State aid
from the start; not only did they not reject it, they applied for it, and
frequently—as you are well aware and all of you remember—not only
obtained State aid, not only set about negotiating protective increases in
tariffs, but turned the negotiations themselves into a weapon of offence
for the purpose of securing every kind of concession from the Spanish
State.

Lecture, Madrid, 9-4-35.

131.   Our modest economic resources are burdened with the support
of an intolerable mass of parasites: bankers who grow rich by lending
other people's money at high rates of interest; owners of great estates
who soullessly and effortlessly charge vast rents for letting them; directors of large Companies who are ten times better remunerated than those
by whose efforts the businesses are run; holders of bonus shares, who in
most cases are being recompensed in perpetuity, or are receiving the re-
wards of intrigue: usurers, money-brokers and middlemen. In order that
this thick layer of idlers may be supported, without their contributing the

slightest addition to the fruits of other people's toil, managers, industrialists, merchants, farmers, fishermen, intellectual workers, artisans and laborers, slaving away with no illusions, are obliged to pare down their scanty means of subsistence. Thus, the standard of living of all the producing classes of Spain, the middle class and the common people, is deplorably low; Spain's problem is one of overproduction by herself, for the exploited Spanish Populace barely consumes at all.

"Arriba," 16-1-36.

132.   How often have you heard men of the Right say: "We live in a new age, we must set up a strong State, we must harmonize capital and labor, we have to seek a corporative form of existence?" I assure you that none of all that means a thing, it is all mere windbaggery. Harmonizing capital and labor . . . is as if I were to say: "I am going to harmonize myself with this chair." Capital—I have already taken up some time in distinguishing capital from private property—is an economic instrument which must serve the entire economy, and hence may not be an instrument for the advantage and privilege of the few who had the luck to get in first. So that when they talk of harmonizing capital and labor, what is meant is to go on nourishing an insignificant privileged minority upon the exertions of all, the exertions of both workers and employers—a fine way of solving the social problem and interpreting economic justice!

Lecture, Madrid, 9-4-35.

V.

ON THE CORPORATIVE AND OTHER FORMS OF STATE

133.   This stuff about the Corporative State is another piece of windbaggery. Mussolini, who has some idea of what the Corporative State means, made a speech when he inaugurated the twenty-two Corporations a few months ago, and in it he said: "This is no more than a starting-point; it is not a destination." Up to the present moment, Corporative organization means nothing else, approximately and on general lines than this: the workmen form one great federation, the employers form another great federation (the givers of work, as they are called in Italy); and between these two great federations the State erects as it were a sort of connecting-piece. As a provisional solution it is all right; but note carefully that this is a device very similar, on a gigantic scale, to our own *Jurados Mixtos.* This device has hitherto maintained the relative position of labor unchanged on the same basis as capitalist economics had fashioned for it; the position still obtains in which one gives employment and the other hires out his own labor in order to live.

Lecture, Madrid, 9-4-35.

134.   Totalitarian States do not exist. There are nations that have found dictators of genius, who have served as substitute for the State: but that is something unique, and in Spain at the present day we shall have to wait for such a genius to arise. Examples of the so-called Totalitarian States are Germany and Italy, and notice that they are not only not similar, but radically opposed to one another: they start from opposite ends. The German one starts from a people's capacity for faith, in its racial instinct. The German people is in an auto ecstasy: Germany is living in an ultra-democracy. Rome, in the other hand, is undergoing the experience of possessing a genius of classic mind, who seeks to mold a people from above. The German movement is of Romantic type, its route, the same as ever; thence sprang the Reformation and even the French Revolution, for the Declaration of the Rights of Man is a tracing of the North-American Constitutions, themselves offspring of German Protestant thought.

Neither Social Democracy nor the attempt to set up a Totalitarian State without a genius would suffice to avert the catastrophe. There is another species of salve, of which we in Spain are prodigal: I refer to the confederations, blocks, and alliances. All of them derive from the postulate that the union of several dwarfs is capable of producing a giant. When faced with this type of remedy, precautions must be taken. And let us not allow ourselves to be taken by surprise by their word spinning. Thus, there are movements of that kind which parade Religion as the first plank of their platform, but only stand to attention when material advantage is involved; which in exchange for a modification in the Agrarian Reform, or a morsel on the Clerical assets, would renounce the Crucifix in schools or the abolition of divorce.

Speech, "Spain and Barbarism," Valladolid, 3-3-35.

VI.
FASCISM

135.   The announcement that José Antonio Primo de Rivera, Leader of *Falange Española de las J.O.N.S.*, was preparing to attend a certain international Fascist Congress now being held at Montreux is completely false. The Leader of the Falange was asked to be present; but he unequivocally declined the invitation, realizing that the truly national character of the movement he leads is inconsistent with even the semblance of international governance.

Moreover, *Falange Española de las J.O.N.S.* is not a Fascist movement. It has certain coincidences with Fascism in essential points which are of universal validity; but it is daily acquiring a clearer outline of its own, and is convinced that by following this path and no other it will find its most fruitful possibilities of development.

Note, composed by José Antonio and published in the Spanish Press,
19-12-34.

136.   Fascism is not a system of tactics-violence. It is an idea-unity. Against Marxism, which affirms the class struggle as a dogma, and against Liberalism, which demands the party struggle as its very machinery of operation. Fascism maintains that there is something above party and above class, something whose nature is permanent, transcendent, supreme: the historical unity called the Patria.

1st Open Letter to Luca de Tena, "ABC," 22-3-33.

137.   Nothing could be further removed from the idle young man about town, the invited guest of life, in which he fulfils no function whatever, than the citizen of the Fascist State, for whom no right is recognized except in virtue of the service he performs in his station. If there is anything that truly deserves to be called a State of Workers, it is the Fascist State.

Ibid.

138.   In a Fascist State it is not the most powerful class or the most numerous party that triumphs: what triumphs is the coordinating principle common to all, the consistent thought of the nation, of which the State is the organ.

Ibid.

139.   Practically none of the objections to Fascism are raised in good faith. They breathe a concealed desire to find an ideological excuse for laziness or cowardice, if not actually for that which is our own outstanding national defect, namely envy, which is capable of squandering the finest things, provided that a fellow creature is thus deprived of an opportunity to shine.

Letter to Julián Pemartín, 2-4-33.

140.   While the Lateran Treaty is being signed in Rome, we here are making allegations that Fascism is anti-Catholic; Fascism, which in Italy, after ninety years of Masonic Liberalism, has restored the Crucifix and religious instruction in the schools. I can understand the uneasiness in Protestant countries where a conflict might be possible between the

national religious tradition and the Catholic fervor of a minority. But in Spain, what can the exaltation of that which is genuinely national lead to, except the discovery of the Catholic factors in our world mission?

Ibid.

VII.
GENERAL CRITIQUE OF SPANISH POLITICS

141.   Spain has long been living a flat, impoverished life, crushed between two millstones which she has not yet succeeded in breaking. The upper one is the lack of all historical ambition and all historical interest; the nether one is the lack of any deep social justice. The lack of historical interest comes from pessimism of thirty or forty years standing, from our failure to find an interest to bind us all together in an effort on behalf of one and the same cause. The lack of social justice comes from the fact that whereas hitherto let us never cease to bless this state of affairs—we have been spared the horrors of heavy industrialization, that heavy industrialization which has let loose on the world one of the greatest of all crises—yet we must none the less realize that our agricultural life, the life of our small towns and villages, is utterly inhuman and inexcusable.

Parliament, 6-6-34.

142.   Our Spain found herself on the one hand saved from the world crisis; but on the other, she lay as if oppressed by a crisis of her own; she was "not herself," but the reasons for her being thus uprooted were not those common to the rest of the world.

Tradition and Revolution, August 1935.

143.   In this place I may not speak in the name of any filial devotion; I must speak as a member of a generation to whose lot it has fallen to live after the Dictatorship, and which, whether willingly or unwillingly, is bound to pass judgment dry-eyed, and if possible from the elevated standpoint of History, on that historical and political phenomenon denoted by the Dictatorship.

Parliament, 6-6-34.

144.   The Dictatorship broke up a constitutional order which obtained at the time of its advent, launched the country on a revolutionary process, and unfortunately, was not able to bring this to a conclusion.

Ibid.

145.   [T]he Dictatorship, which subverted a constitutional order, was not bound to justify itself by a number of juridical requirements. . . . Not that this means that it did not have to justify itself as a historical and political event.

Ibid.

146.   [T]he Dictatorship . . . failed, tragically and magnificently, because it was unable to carry out its revolutionary task.

Ibid.

147.   General Primo de Rivera . . . was not understood by those who imagined they loved him, and was not loved by those who could have understood him.

In other words: if the intellectuals, who had long been desirous of a revolutionary change in Spain, either from below or from above, had understood him, the revolution could have been achieved. By them, he was not understood; and, on the other hand, the people who loved him were those who for one reason or another had not the slightest desire to achieve any revolution at all.

Ibid.

148.   The dwarfs have prevailed over the giant. They put nets around his feet and threw him to the ground. Then they tortured him by pinpricks. And he, who was good, sensitive, simple; he, who was not armor-plated against the sight of want; he, who because he was very much of a man, very "human," enjoyed and suffered as children do, bowed his head one morning and raised it no more.

Today is the hour of the dwarfs. What revenge they take for the silence to which he reduced them! How they agitate, how they dribble, how they turn indecent somersaults in their envenomed jubilation! Everything must be flung away! Not even a trace to remain of all that he did! And the most ridiculous of all the dwarfs, the pedants, smile ironically.

"The hour of the Dwarfs," 1931.

149.   The Dictatorship which was incarnated in a really extraordinary man, in a man (as I am sure no-one will deny) possessing what—no less a person than Ortega y Gasset, one of his most constant opponents—has described as a warm heart, accompanied by a finely tempered spirit and the clearest of heads; possessing a power of intuition and divination and an understanding such as few men are endowed with, found itself short of one thing, without which it is impossible for a regime to go ahead: the Dictatorship was short of dialectical grace.

This fact, at that time, was perfectly excusable.

Parliament, 6-6-34.

150.　The Spanish Monarchy had been a historical executive instrument for the attainment of one of the greatest of universal ends. It had founded and maintained an empire, and it had founded and maintained it precisely through that which constituted its prime virtue: the virtue of representing unity of command. Without unity of command one gets nowhere. But the Monarchy ceased to be a unity of command quite a long time ago. By Philip III, the King no longer ruled; the King, continued to be the outward symbol, but the exercise of power fell into the hands of strong men and of Ministers: of Lerma, of Olivares, of Aranda, of Godoy. When Charles IV came to the throne, the Monarchy was now no more than a shadow without substance. The Monarchy which had started in the camp had retired to the seclusion of the Cortes. The Spanish people is implacable in its realism; the Spanish people, which demands that its patron Saints shall bring rain when it is needed, and turns their images back to front on the altar if they don't bring it; the Spanish people, I repeat, did not understand this shadow of a Monarchy without power. That is why that shadow fell from its place on April the 14th 1931, without even a platoon of the Lifeguards putting up a fight.

Speech, Madrid, 19-5-35.

151.　[I]n the matter of the Monarchy we cannot allow ourselves to be swayed for a moment either by wishful longing or by cherished ill will. We must confront the problem of the Monarchy with the implacable strictness of men who witness a decisive event in the course of the days that go to make up history. Did the Spanish Monarchy, the ancient, glorious Spanish Monarchy, fall because it had come to the end of its cycle, because its mission was ended; or was the Spanish Monarchy overthrown while it still possessed fertility for the future . . . ? We realize, without a shadow of irreverence, without a shadow of ill-will, without a shadow of dislike, indeed many of us with a thousand reasons for feelings of affection; we realize that the Spanish Monarchy had completed its cycle, was left without substance, and fell off like a dead husk, on April 14th 1931. We record its fall with all the emotion it deserves, and we have the highest respect for monarchists who, believing it still capable of a future, urge people to regain it; but we ourselves, much as it grieves us, and although there may rise within some of our hearts some sentimental reserve or some not unworthy regret, we cannot fling the fresh urge of the youth that follows us into the attempt to recover an institution, that we regard as gloriously dead.

Ibid.

152.   [T]he Spanish Republic, whose legitimacy I imagine nobody is going to question, was not born in the municipal elections of April 12th. . . . When the revolutionary Committee announced in the Gazette the fact that they had taken over power, the gentlemen forming this revolutionary Committee signed their decree of April 15th, not as elected councilors but as members of the revolutionary Committee, which had in a revolutionary manner imposed their authority on the Spanish body politic, as the disproportionate outcome of some municipal elections.

Parliament, 6-6-34.

153.   Seldom can there have been a more propitious moment, with one chapter concluded, to start a new and a great chapter in our country's history. . . . There was no resentment to be cherished, no justice to be executed, almost no tears to dry. Ahead stretched bright hopes for a whole people: you yourselves remember the rejoicings of April 14th. The rejoicing of April 14th, once again, was the Spanish people's rediscovery of an old longing for their suspended revolution. The Spanish people have been in need of their revolution, and they thought they had got it on the 14th of April 1931; they thought they had got it, because it seemed to them that this date was handing them the promise of two great things that they had long been pining for: first, the restoration of a collective national spirit, and secondly, the erection of a material human basis of common social life among Spaniards.

Speech Madrid, 19-5-35.

154.   On that April morning there were neither Socialists nor Liberals, neither workers nor bourgeois. We were all one: a multitude full of hope, ready and willing to be molded by the hands of the best men amongst us. How did it come about that we people who for years had been burning with widely diverse ambitions should have fused together in one single state of emotion?

What had occurred was simply this: as always when a high spiritual temperature is attained, the vegetable growth of all the programs had gone up in smoke, the material aspirations had been burned away, and there surged up into view, stronger than any distorted notions, the warm, deep-buried vein that lies within us all, perhaps without our knowing it. There shone forth once again the religious, mystical quality of the great popular manifestations: it was not a matter of belief in this or in that, in this man or in that man, but of belief in this joyous moment newly arrived. The people no longer trusted to the virtue of this program or that, but to its implicit certainty that it had achieved a miraculous capacity for divination. Dissensions with one another, which until yesterday had seemed like mountain ranges, vanished. You might almost say that we had learnt to fly without knowing how, and that from the heights to which we had soared, everything looked tiny. If the 14th of April had held no more than the programs and the men that we knew, little could have been hoped for from it. What mattered was that other something, that gaiety of the 14th of April, which, being as it was so indefinite in its expression, concealed a deeper exactitude than that of all the programs, namely this: a fervid aspiration towards the recovery of Spain's spiritual unity upon a fresh basis of physical existence for the people. Patria and Justice for a much-suffered people. "Nation and Work," as Ortega y Gasset later said.

Youth Out in the Cold, "Arriba," 7-11-35.

155.   On April 14th, 1931, occurred a manifestation of popular joy similar to that of September 13th, 1923. On April 14th, a thousand-year-old institution was overthrown . . . what so filled with joy those who rejoiced on that date was the hope that once more we had arrived at the moment for the breaking of the upper millstone of lack of ambition and historical mission, and the lower one of lack of social justice. The revolution of April 14th seemed to hold out the promise, as regards the historical record, of restoring to Spain a common interest and a common undertaking. . . . And later, as regards the social background, the revolution of April 14th did bring no less, and this indeed was its most far reaching and interesting contribution: the inclusion of the Socialists in a Governmental task that was not exclusively proletarian.

Parliament, 6-6-34.

156.   Every time the revival of a common national ambition has apparently been glimpsed, it has quickly been frustrated by the strife of party against party. The last occasion was the 14th of April three years ago. At that time, and at the cost regretted by many of losing a thousand-year-old institution, an opportunity full of joyous collective hope, seemed, in the eyes of nearly all of us, to be arising.

A Manifesto to Spain. "F.E.," 26-4-34.

157.   The men of April 14th seemed to be returning to patriotism once more, and returning by the best of all ways: the bitter way of criticism. Therein lay their promise of fruitfulness.

Speech, Madrid, 19-5-35.

158.   The first Government of the Republic was born with a tinge of brass-band mediocrity about it; it was a very worthy foretaste of the ones we have after 1933.

"Arriba," 31-10-35.

159.   In the eyes of history, the men of the 14th of April bear the terrible responsibility of having once again defrauded the Spanish revolution. The men of the 14th of April did not do what the 14th of April promised.

Speech, Madrid, 19-5-35.

160.   We have witnessed the sight of a Parliament which, convinced that electoral victory empowered it to do whatever it saw fit, did so indeed, even up to the point of crushing the rest of humanity.

Lecture, Madrid, 9-4-35.

161.   (The Republic), instead of laying itself out to better the people's lot by a generous policy, excited it by aggressive propaganda and then left it empty-handed—no less hungry than before, and angrier. A crude and embittered Marxism prevented the national and the social from being harmonized. Social policy in many respects took on an insolent frame of mind, an air of conqueror's arrogance. Children in schools began raising the clenched fist, and Socialist workmen began looking about them in the street with the haughtiness of people who, if they tolerate the rest of mankind's existence at all, do so out of pure condescension. A Russian, Asiatic, despotic atmosphere brooded over everything. The dictatorship of the proletariat was beginning to loom ahead.

Youth Out in the Cold, "Arriba," 7-11-35.

162.   [T]here is nothing that corrodes a regime so much as the seeking to elucidate the responsibilities of the preceding regimes.

Parliament, 6-6-34.

163.   His (Azaña's) appearance seemed to augur a change of style. Azaña was not a man of the people: he was one of an intellectual minority, a select and disdainful writer, an exacting, cold, precise, original dialectician. From the moment of his appearance before the footlights in the blare of public activity, he had shown himself to be, apparently, free from the general mediocrity and completely contemptuous of applause. He was, undoubtedly, an exceptionally interesting political specimen: a man who had reached the highest post of command practically without compromise or effort, in a singularly auspicious period, and who was preparing the machinery for remolding the people to his own choice. The old radicals and radical socialists had nothing fresh to reveal; this reserved, mysterious member of the Athenaeum might perhaps, carry out some surprising experiments. What was the reason for Azaña's failure? It may be that some old personal embitterment or other prevailed over

his qualifications of statesmanship. It may be that those external and outstanding qualifications of statesmanship were squandered in futility for
lack of any fructifying breath of enthusiasm. "Azaña, or, Infertility"
might be the title of an essay to be written upon him. A complete and
accurate set of levers and cogwheels but no engine. Azaña gave himself
over to a kind of aestheticism in politics which ended up as aestheticism
in cruelty. His best pieces of work, those that were not mere aggressive
blunderings, were useless filigree. Regarding history as if it were a sort
of sport, he would play the game for its own sake and not for the result
achieved: he was reminiscent, for example, of those champion runners
who do their running not in order to reach a goal since nothing awaits
them when they get there but for the sake of the distance covered. His
policy was thus a monstrosity. For those unable to appreciate the pedantic aestheticism for which it served as a cloak, it was a kind of diabolical,
unintelligible torture. Spain passed through the hands of this dictator as
through those of an Asiatic masseur, half fascinated and half tormented;
on the day he went out of office, she experienced the relief of someone
who can rest once more.

"Azaña," "Arriba," 31-10-35.

164.   [T]he political reproach that can be flung at Señor Azaña, the
real and serious charge that can be preferred against Señor Azaña, is this:
Señor Azaña had in his hands one of those opportunities which descend
on peoples every fifty, sixty, or hundred years; Señor Azaña could without difficulty have carried out the Spanish revolution, the unpostponable
and essential Spanish revolution.

Parliament, 21-3-35.

165.   Azaña will govern again. He will be brought back this time with
a revolutionary roar—even if the roaring goes, on around the polls—on
the back of the mob who listened to his voice on the 20th of October.
Once again he will have in the hollow of his hand the caesarian opportunity of fulfilling—even in the teeth of the shouting masses—the revolutionary destiny which will have twice elected him. Once again Spain,
broad and virginal with all her fears and her hopes, will put him in the
way of mastering her secret. Only if he hits upon this will he have a message strong enough to shout above the noise of the Red mob who will
have raised him on high. But Azaña will not hit upon the secret: he will
give himself over to the mob, which will turn him into a servile ragamuf-
fin, or else he will try to oppose the mob without possessing the authority
for so great a task, and the mob will smash him and will smash Spain as
well.

"Azaña," "Arriba," 31-10-35.

166.   If at the end of four days or six days after the 6th of October 1934[6] the Spanish State had come to the conclusion that Don Manuel Azaña was a representative opposed to, and incompatible with, the State itself, and had had him shot by a firing squad, it is quite possible that a legal injustice would have been committed, but it is clear that historical justice would have been served.

Parliament, 21-3-35.

167.   "Right" and "Left" are barren and incomplete values. The Right, through seeking to ignore the distress and urgent economic demands of the times, end up by depriving their religious and patriotic appeals of all human validity. The Left, through closing the minds of the masses to what is spiritual and national, end up by degrading economic conflict into the savagery of wild beasts. Today two total concepts of the world stand facing one another; whichever wins will finally break off the customary alternation. Either victory will go to the spiritual, Western, Christian, Spanish concept of life with all the service and sacrifice it involves, but with all the individual dignity and national honor it possesses, else victory will go to the materialist and Russian concept of life, which beyond subjecting Spaniards to the savage yoke of a Red Army and a ruthless policy, will disintegrate Spain into local republics.

Sheet written in the dungeons of Security Police Headquarters,
14-3-36.

168.   Underneath these superficial terms Right and Left, lies something deeper hidden. The essence of these attitudes of "right-wing" and "left-wing" might be thus summarized: those of the "right wing" are those who think that the main purpose of the State justifies any individual sacrifice, and that any personal interest should be subordinated to the collective one; those of the "left wing," on the contrary make their primary affirmation that of the individual, and to this all else is subordinated: the paramount thing is his interest, and nothing that assails it is considered legitimate.

But, according to these definitions, would not Communism belong to the Right? Does Communism belong to the Right? For Communism subordinates everything to the interest of the State; in no country has there ever existed less freedom than in Russia; in none has there ever been a more oppressive suffocation of the individual by the State. But it is known that the ultimate goal of Communism is a Stateless and classless organization, a perfect anarchy and equality. Such has been declared by

---

[6] The Separatist armed revolts in Catalonia and Asturias, acts of high treason in which Azaña was implicated—Translator.

the Communist leaders: after a hard stage of dictatorial rigor, an approximately anarchistic collectivism.

In muddled periods like the one we live in, the outlines of these two
constants get blurred. So, it comes about that the arch-conservatives feel
themselves "left-wingers," in other words individualists, when the question of defending their interests arises. Both the Left and the Right get
jumbled together and contradict each other, because they have lost sight
of the fundamental idea in their respective constants.

Lecture "State, Individual, Freedom," 28-3-35.

169.   The Right wishes to preserve the Patria, to preserve unity, to
preserve authority; but it ignores this anguish of the man, the individual,
the fellow-creature who has nothing to eat.

Lecture, Madrid, 9-4-35.

170.   The Right is the attempt to perpetuate an economic system even
though it be an unjust one, and the Left is at heart the desire to overthrow
an economic organization even though in its overthrow many good
things should be ruined.

Speech, Madrid, 29-10-33.

171.   The parties of the Left do see man, but they see him in an uprooted state. The common factor of all the Left elements is concern for
the individual as against all historic architecture and all political architecture, as if man and these were contradictory terms. Hence "Leftism"
is a solvent, it is corrosive; it is ironical, and endowed though it is with a
brilliant assembly of intellects, is nevertheless very good at destruction
and seldom much good at construction.

Lecture, Madrid, 9-4-35.

172.   Both of them (Right and Left) cloak their insufficiency with
verbiage. The one lot invoke the Patria without feeling or service at all;
the others minimize their disregard and indifference towards the basic
problem of every man by formulae which in reality are nothing but mean-
ingless verbal effrontery.

Ibid.

173.   It is just as well that the ballot-boxes look so like the drums used
in the State Lottery. It is all the same whether one ball rolls into a hole
first, or whether one handful of paper slips vanquishes another. The thing
is decided by whatever imp is in charge of the hazards of the lottery; that
is, any old spirit, good or evil, whether of justice, revenge, or hysteria.
Pure chance: a good joke at a candidate's expense can rob him of victory

at the eleventh hour. The itch to get rid of an irritating Government can lead a people to overthrow a thousand things.

"F.E.," 7-12-33.

174.   Yet there are people who believe that nothing less than the victory of counter revolution has been won in this lottery. A lot of people are feeling very pleased about it. Once more Spain is trying to scar the wound over prematurely, to close the mouth of the wound without clearing up the trouble inside. Put simply: she is trying to write off a revolution as settled while the revolution is still alive within, more or less covered over by this fragile skin that has emerged from the ballot-boxes.

Ibid.

175.   [A]s for the Populist[7] school, what would you expect of it? The Populist school is like one of those great German factories in which they produce ersatz substitutes for almost every genuine article in existence. For example, there arises the world phenomenon of Socialism, there arises the bloodthirsty, violent, genuine drive of the Socialist masses. Immediately the Populist school—rich in card indexes and cautious young men, well-endowed to be sure with prudence and good breeding, but resembling more than anything else those trained in the most refined Masonic school—produces an ersatz Socialism and organizes something calling itself Christian Democracy; against People's Palaces, it sets People's Palaces; against card-indexes, card-indexes; against social legislation, social legislation of its own. It becomes skilled in writing manifestoes on profit-sharing, on workmen's pensions, on a thousand other pretty things. The only thing that happens is that the real workers do not enter these charming Populist cages. Next, Fascism arises in the world with its values of struggle and resurgence and protest of oppressed peoples against adverse conditions, with its train of martyrs and its hopes of glory. Immediately out comes the Populist party and off it goes somewhere, let us say to El Escorial so that nobody will think they are being referred to, and organizes a youth demonstration, with banners, with travelling expenses paid, and with everything that could be desired except the youthful valor, revolutionary and robust, which the young Fascist possessed.

176.   The Right have got nothing from their victory except purely selfish and Conservative results. They have repealed the Agrarian Reform Act, which was a bad law, not in order to substitute a good one for

---

[7] "Populist" school: from "*Acción Popular*," an organization dependent on the C. E. D. A. (Spanish Confederation of independent Right-Wing Parties); leader, Gil Robles.—Translator.

it, but to replace it with a cynical sham which will not give the Spanish peasants any land inside of two centuries. They contemplate undismayed the revival of starvation wages; they devote little more than verbiage to the problem of unemployment. . . . In a word, they stand by with folded arms in face of the survival of a dismal, poverty-stricken, unhealthy, harsh, and desperate standard of life.

Youth Out in the Cold, "Arriba," 7-11-35.

177.   If the Right which was victorious in 1933 had had any message to bring to Spain, the would-be Caesar of the April revolution would never have reared his head again. But it would be idle to seek precedents for a clumsier piece of blundering than that committed by the Spanish Right. Instead of obliterating the memory of the enemy by a sound and far reaching piece of work for all to see, they have done nothing but keep the memory of the enemy alive by an endless campaign of crude and ugly defamation, and slumber in a deadly sloth unpardonable at a revolutionary moment like the present. The policy of the second biennium (the stupid one, as it has also been called in these columns) has been one of barren conservation of every obstacle in the way of a brighter outlook for the future. A hybrid policy: not altogether secularist, so as not to strike at the Catholics; not informed by religious feeling, so as not to annoy the old priest devouring radicals; not generous in the social sphere, so as to keep in with the selfishness of the old county squirearchy; and not unprovided in with an occasional Platonic declaration of the Christian-democrat variety, from the pen of that restless canonist Señor Jimenez.

"Azaña," "Arriba," 31-10-35.

178.   A peaceful siesta. That is what is sought, as a maximal program, by three-fourths of this Spain whose Constitution has renounced war and whose vitiated palate has lost its ancient taste for the heroic.

While Spain sleep her Siesta, "Haz," 19-7-35.

179.   You would think that there was hanging over our country the curse of never having become a clear-cut, established reality, but only an everlasting project of a reality, forever in the unstable stage of a rough draft.   A Manifesto to Spain, "F.E.," 26-4-34.

180.   The Left-Wing insolence of the Constituent Parliament was an evil thing; but the complacent young-man-about-town atmosphere of this one, the inane titterings of the present majority in face of Spain's distress is not the sort of thing we were seeking either. We young men, stirred by the urges of the spirit, free from the crude egoism of the old political

bosses, what we were longing to see was a Spain great, and just, a Spain with an order and a faith. This is not it, not this.

Youth Out in the Cold, "Arriba," 7-11-35.

181.   Don't you notice how we are breathing an atmosphere like that of the last days of 1930, when we could all feel the nearness of the gulf ahead? The thing is dying, and it is dying after a whole life of sterility.

Speech, Madrid. 17-11-35.

182.   When all is said and done, if there were nothing more than that going on, I mean the finish of the hastily erected shack, whose pulling down we have all foreseen and many of us have looked forward to, then we should have nothing else to do but to look on. However, it is not just that. It is that on the eve of the collapse we are bound to be appalled by the question. What is going to happen afterwards?

Ibid.

183.   Local separatism is the decadence that arises at the exact moment when men forget that their Patria is not the obvious physical thing that can be perceived even in the most primitive state of spontaneity.

Speech, Valladolid, 4-3-34.

184.   Is the loss of unity—territorial, spiritual, historical—less evident here than anywhere else? It is possible to say in any and every case that one should wait until things get worse. But if the matter can be attended to earlier, what purpose is served by waiting till the situation becomes desperate? Especially during the gestation period of a Socialist dictatorship, organized from within the Government, and calculated, if not mismanaged, to put Spain into a position from which it would be most difficult to retreat.

185.   It has been said that autonomy is coming to mean the recognizing of a region's personality; that autonomy is being won precisely by those regions which are most highly differentiated, by the regions showing the most marked local culture. I should be grateful, and I believe Spain would be grateful too, if we all gave some thought to this point. If we grant autonomy as the reward of differentiation, we run the very grave risk that this autonomy may serve as a stimulus towards still deeper differentiation. If autonomy is to be won by distinguishing oneself by deeply marked characteristics from the rest of the lands of Spain, then in conferring autonomy we run the risk of extending an invitation to deepen these differences between the region and the rest of Spain. Accordingly

my opinion is that when a region applies for autonomy, instead of en-
quiring whether it possesses more or less strongly marked characteristics, what we ought to enquire into is how strongly rooted in its heart the
consciousness of a unity of destiny is; for, if the consciousness of unity
of destiny is strongly rooted in the collective soul of a region, little or no
danger is incurred by our giving such a region the freedom to organize
its internal life in this or that fashion.

186.   A region has come of age when it has acquired so strong a consciousness of the unity of its destiny with that of the common Patria that
this unity no longer runs any risk from the weakening of administrative
ties.

"Spain is Irrevocable," "F. E.," 19-7-34.

187.   All who have a feeling for Spain say "Long live Catalonia!"
And long live all her sister lands in this admirable, indestructible glorious
mission, from which we have inherited so many centuries of effort in the
name of Spain!

Parliament, 4-1-34.

188.   [W]hen we use the name of Spain, there is something within us
that stirs us, something far above any desire to vex a political regime,
and far above any wish to vex a land so noble, so great, so famous and
so beloved as the land of Catalonia.

Ibid.

189.   We must study Catalonia afresh, we must observe Catalonia at
our leisure with all affection, with all understanding, but without haste
or any preconceived answers, in order to see whether she is truly welded
to the sense of unity with the destinies of the nation.

Ibid., 30-11-34.

190.   The Catalonian Generalitat was merely one episode in the
whole campaign of subversion by which an attempt was made to complete the annihilation of Spain.

191.   [T]here came an attempted coup which, fortunately for the Government and for everyone, appeared in an anti-national guise; it was stupid enough to raise a separatist standard, by which it provoked an in-
stinctive feeling of repulsion even in the most extreme popular sectors.
The proletarian side of the attempt lost caste through this inhibiting
cause; for a Spanish man of the people, however much internationalist

propaganda he may have got into his head, is always loth to rally to the anti-national banner of separatism.

Parliament, 25-1-35.

192.   The revolutionaries had the mystical sense—Satanic, if you like, but mystical—of their revolution, and that mystical sense of revolution neither society nor the Government was able to confront with the mystical sense of a duty permanent and binding in all circumstances.

Ibid., 6-11-34.

193.   In this their duty of putting down the rebellion instantly, of bringing it not cruelly but cleanly and quickly to an end, the Government has utterly failed. Had this been fulfilled, another task awaited the Government, namely, to find out what internal wrongs and lack of consistency or internal justice had permitted a daring minority to plunge into an attempt to seize power by force. The Government ought to have made this examination of conscience, as indeed it should always be made in the day after a victory, so as to find out in what respects the vanquished may have been in the right, and to prevent others from trying to do what the vanquished have failed to achieve. This the Government gets daily further from doing; every day the Government takes less and less account of the reasons for its own existence.

Ibid., 25-1-35.

194.   The Government knows perfectly well just how much support of every kind rallied around it in the occasion of October 7th. It is not necessary to recall again, as I have recalled more than once already, how it was actually the youthful impetuosity of the people who are my companions and followers that made the first demonstration in the Puerta del Sol with myself at their head; but, to be precise, it was for the purpose of shouting in the ear of the Government just this: "You have come to a decisive moment; you have a decisive moment before you, from which there can emerge unending consequences for Spain!"

Ibid.

195.   Neither Spanish State nor Spanish society would have defended themselves vigorously against the revolution, had there not entered into play the factor which always looks unforeseen to us, but which never fails to make its appearance on historic occasions: namely, the hidden genius of Spain, which now as ever is housed within military uniforms, uniforms of tough young soldieries, splendid officers, staunch veterans and ready volunteers, has once again, now as ever, given Spain back her unity and her peace.

Ibid. 6-11-34.

196.   [T]his heroic military vein the same as ever has saved us. This heroic military vein must once more regain its paramount position.

Ibid.

197.   The men of Spain who have been trying to penetrate into the innermost vitals of our living reality in order to destroy it have used Catalonia in their game as a docile pawn to be sacrificed. The ringleaders of the disintegrative, suicidal and barren revolution we have suffered set up the Catalans as propitiatory sacrificial dummies of straw, and turned to account the anarchistic, blood-thirsty, farcical lunacy of a senseless Catalan breakaway, whose compass-course had changed at the last moment from that of common crime to that of embittered and underhand speculation, charged with the darkest and most erroneous particularism.

198.   The victory over the first armed rising of the Generalidad contained enough historical solidity to last half a century. It was squandered. "Expediency" continued to dictate lukewarm solutions and dilatory negotiations. The brilliant, clean-cut suppression of the rising gave way to an interminable labyrinth of postponement and haggling. Even now, a year later, we have before us what is called the "liquidation of the events of October." The State is giving things back piecemeal, without any guarantee of the preservation of national unity. As for Socialism, instead of being dismantled and replaced by something else, it is being exacerbated on the one hand and allowed to be encouraged on the other.

Youth Out in the Cold, "Arriba," 7-11-35.

199.   Squandered opportunities are just those which have always opened the way towards national revolutions. The squandering of Vittorio Veneto led to the March on Rome; the squandering of October 7th may well lead to our National Revolution, in the ranks of which I enlist.

Parliament, 6-11-34.

200.   The night before last, two young Falangists were murdered in Seville. Their names are Eduardo Rivas and Jerónimo de la Rosa. Were they "playboys of Fascism"? One was a humble painter; the other, a poor student who had a job with the Railway Company. Had they joined the Falange to defend capitalism? What had they to do with capitalism; if anything, they were rather sufferers from its defects. They joined the Falange because they realized that the whole world is going through a spiritual crisis, that the harmony between the destiny of men and the destiny of communities has broken down. They were not anarchists: they were

not in favor of sacrificing the destiny of the community to that of the individual; they were not advocates of any form of all absorbing totalitarian State, and therefore they did not wish to see the individual destiny disappear in that of the community. They believed that the way to regain harmony between the individual and the community was this union of the syndical idea with the national, which defends itself, against the lying tongues of those who misrepresent, and against the deaf ears of those who will not hear, in the Falangist system of ideas. So, they joined the ranks of the Falange, and they went out into the streets of Seville two nights ago to put up posters advertising a legally permitted newspaper. And while they were posting the bills on a wall they were shot down in cold blood; one fell dead on the pavement, and the other died in hospital a few hours later.

Parliament, 8-11-35.

201.   In the streets of Seville disputes between political bands have been settling themselves with firearms for more than a year. The Falange is proud to say that not once has it been the initiator of an attack. The Falange can say that not once has it been found guilty of a single attack. One day a working man belonging to the Falange is killed; the whole city points to the Communist party as the instigator of the murder; not a single Communist headquarters is closed down, not one known Communist is punished, nothing is done.

But a few days later, when two or three attacks on Falangists have occurred, a number of Communists are shot in the doorway of their headquarters. Without any further enquiries, the Governor of Seville puts in prison, not those presumed responsible who have already cleared themselves in Court—but fifteen Falange leaders, fining each of them 5,000 pesetas and closing down every headquarters in the Province. So unjust was the punishment that merely after one conversation with myself the Minister for Home Affairs, as he then was, Don Manuel Portela Valladares, quashed all the fines and ordered all the men to be released.

But again a man is killed, and a few hours later a second, both belonging to the Falange. It would seem a clear case of reprisal; nevertheless, the Communist headquarters are not closed down, not a single Communist is arrested, not a single Communist is fined. . . .

This state of affairs, which would in any event be . . . a criminal complicity with one of the parties, and with that party which has always initiated the aggression, becomes far more serious . . . in the present circumstances. There is being fomented in Spain, with greater and greater violence, an appallingly menacing revolutionary situation, appallingly menacing for the traditionalists, and for you too, the liberal-bourgeois, for the Republicans of the Left. I have in my hand, Mr.

Minister for Home Affairs, a non-clandestine publication. It is a book called October, which I was able to buy quite openly. It bears the imprint of the press it came from; on the flyleaf is stated the publisher who produced it, and as if that were not enough, on the opposite page it is declared to be a book of resolutions and policies of the Socialist Youth groups and issued under the official aegis of their President, our fellow Member of Parliament, Don Carlos Hernández Zancajo. In this book, on page 160, the theses of the Federation of Socialist Youth Groups are printed . . . they are these: "For the Bolshevization of the Socialist Party. Expulsion of the "reformist." Elimination of "centre-party" men from key positions. Abandonment of the Second International. For the transformation of Party"—note this—"into a centralized system provided with an illegal organization." This is not something stated in a clandestine publication; the proposal to form an illegal organization is announced by a recognized political body in a book that anybody can purchase for three pesetas. "For the political unification of the Spanish proletariat in the Socialist Party. For anti-militarist propaganda. For the unification of the syndicalist movement. For the overthrow of the bourgeoisie [in which you are included] and the triumph of the revolution in the form of the proletarian dictatorship. . . . For the rebuilding of the national working-class movement on the lines of the Russian Revolution. . . . The Socialist Youth considers the leader and initiator of this revolutionary resurgence to be Comrade Largo Caballero."

This is the tone of the revolutionary movement that is in preparation; this is the thing, more and more harsh, more and more hostile, more and more stark, that is brewing beneath all these more or less unconvincing coalitions of Socialists with leftwing Republicans, this is it: a dictatorship of Asiatic, Russian type, without the least vestige of that sentimental feeling that quickened the working-class movements in their initial stages. This is what is being prepared in Spain, this is the thing that is snarling beneath the indifference of Spain. . . .

Therefore, I do not demand for these two fallen comrades of mine the mere respect I should demand towards any fellow-citizen, however near to me, who had been murdered in the street; I demand your admiration and your gratitude that amidst the criminal heedlessness of almost everyone there are humble men in the firing-line, falling one after another, dying one after another, in defense of a Spain that perhaps is not worthy of their sacrifice.

Ibid.

202.   [T]he declaration, embodied in the Constitution, that Spain renounces war. What does that mean? If it is a mere piece of stupidity with nothing else behind it, that is the author's business. If it means that Spain

has the intention of staying neutral in future wars, then that declaration ought to have been followed up by an increase in our land, sea, and air forces, for a nation with all her flanks exposed and situated in one of the danger spots of Europe cannot decide even on her own neutrality if she is not able to make herself respected. Only the strong can be honorably neutral. I do not know whether the authors of that expression were seeking to impose on us a dishonorable neutrality.

Speech, Madrid, 19-5-35.

203.   Spain has been carrying out French international policy for four years now, moving in the international orbit of France. That Spain should develop an international policy in agreement with friendly powers is nothing surprising. But in international affairs nations never give without receiving something and France, whose international policy we serve, treats us badly in trade treaties, relegates us to a level of inferiority in Tangier, and arranges the Mediterranean regime behind our backs, as if we ourselves were not a Mediterranean nation; in other words, all we get from serving the French international policy throughout the world is the satisfaction of some pedantic Minister's, or Ambassador's, personal vanity.

Ibid.

204.   [T]he politics of the Mediterranean are being calmly arranged at public talks held by a Premier and a Foreign Minister, and it is at a moment like this that we are left—as if we were an island in the Pacific—without the least indication that the Government is taking any trouble to claim a seat in the name of Spain in order to have a voice in the organization and polities of the Mediterranean.

Parliament, 25-1-35.

205.   Once all possibility of a modus vivendi has broken down, the Cortes will have to be dissolved. A general election will mean the handing of the country over to strife between two equal and ruthless factions, the Right and the Left. Who will have right on their side in this strife?

To find that out it is necessary to enquire what is the Left, and what is the Right, in Spain.

Letter to a Spanish Officer, 1935.

206.   The constitutional order now in force can no longer support its own weight. In order to remain alive the State is obliged to have recourse to subterfuges that place it outside the normal working of its institutions. What we have now is no longer that state of war that has become endemic, with its attendant train of closures, suppression of newspapers,

political detentions and all the rest of it; it is the formation of a Government which came to birth under a Parliamentary regime, but would not survive half an hour in Parliament; a Government which, in order to enjoy a fugitive illusion of life, is obliged to keep the Cortes closed up to the maximum time-limit sanctioned by the Constitution.

Ibid.

207.   The present trustees of the Popular Front, in compliance with a plan formed abroad, are systematically stripping Spanish life of everything that might put up a resistance to the invasion of the barbarians.

Letter to the Spanish Armed Forces, written secretly in the Model
Prison, Madrid, 4-5-36.

208.   In this respect, the victory of the Popular Front is not good for us. Neither would the victory of the Right have been good. We should have reached such a stage of utilitarian degradation that spiritual values would have tended to become completely suffocated, or, worse still, perverted into mere verbiage, burlesque and sham. This process of degradation was already well advanced by the eve of the elections. Their victory on this occasion would have been the triumph of capitalism in a conspiracy of all its worst aspects. The Falange would have suffered more, spiritually, in such a quagmire of peace than in the stark warfare that confronts us today.

In Stormy Weather. 1936.

209.   The "watchwords" come from abroad, from Moscow. See how they prevail among quite different peoples. See how in France, in obedience of Soviet orders, the Popular Front has been transformed to the same model as in Spain. See how—as we are informed by those who know these moves—there has been a truce in this country up to the exact date when the French elections concluded, and how on the very day when disorders in Spain could no longer influence the decision of the French electorate, arson and massacre have broken out anew.

Letter to the Armed Forces of Spain, 4-5-36.

210.   The "slogans" you have heard in the streets: not only "Long live Russia!" and "Russia, yes! Spain, no!", but even the shameless and monstrous cry of "Death to Spain!" For shouting "Death to Spain!" no one has been punished so far; yet for shouting "Long live Spain!" there are hundreds of people in prison. If this appalling truth were not public property, one would not dare to write it for fear of being taken for a liar.

Ibid.

211.   The "aims of the revolution" are clear enough. The *Agrupacion Socialista* of Madrid, in the official program it has published claims for the different regions and colonies an unlimited right of self-determination, even up to the point of declaring themselves independent.

Ibid.

212.   The "feeling" of the movement now coming to the fore is fundamentally anti-Spanish. It is hostile to the Patria. It scorns chastity by encouraging the collective prostitution of young working girls at those country festivals where every sort of impurity is practiced; it undermines the family, which has been supplanted in Russia by free love, by collective eating-houses, by facilities for divorce and abortion (haven't you recently heard Spanish girls shouting, "Children, yes! Husbands, no!"), and it disowns that sentiment of honor which has always inspired the actions of Spaniards even in the humblest circumstances. Today every villainy reigns in Spain: men are slain in cowardly fashion, a hundred against one; the truth is falsified by the authorities; defamation is inflicted by filthy libels, and the mouths of the injured parties are stopped so that they cannot defend themselves; the traitor and the informer are rewarded. . . . Is this Spain? Is this the people of Spain? You would think we were living in a nightmare, or that the ancient Spanish people—serene, courageous, generous—had been replaced by a frenzied and degenerate plebs, drugged with Communist propaganda pamphlets. Only in the worst moments of the nineteenth century has our people known times like these, and they themselves lacked the acuteness of today.

Ibid.

213.   The Army is above all the safeguard of what is permanent; for that reason, it ought not to get involved in incidental struggles. But when it is a permanent element itself that is endangered, when what is in jeopardy is the very permanence of the Patria (which may, for example, even suffer the loss of its own unity, if things take a certain course), the Army has thing for it but to take counsel and make its choice. If it holds aloof, through a merely outward interpretation of its duty, it runs the risk of finding itself left overnight with nothing to serve. When faced with prospects of a final collapse, the Armed Forces can serve that which is permanent in one way only: by rescuing it with their own arms.

Letter to a Spanish Officer, 1935.

214.   Can there still be anyone among you, Spanish soldiers and officers, of land, sea and air, who proclaims that the Services are not interested in polities? Such a thing could and should be said when politics pursued their course between one party and another. The sword of the

fighting man had no call to settle their conflicts, which were, for their part, thoroughly undistinguished. But today we do not find ourselves faced with a merely internal conflict. What is at stake is the very existence of Spain as an entity and as a unity. The present peril is precisely equivalent to that of a foreign invasion. And this is no rhetorical figure of speech: the foreignness of the movement that is laying siege to Spain is betrayed by its watchwords, by its slogans, by its aims and by its sentiments.

Letter to the Armed Forces, 4-5-36.

215.   Soldiers: without the aid of your forces it would be a task of titanic difficulty for us to be victorious in the struggle. If your forces should be hesitant, it is certain the enemy would win. Weigh your awful responsibility. Whether Spain shall continue in being depends upon you. Consider whether this does not oblige you to go over the heads of bought or cowardly leaders, and to rise superior to hesitation and peril. The enemy is wary and is banking on your indecision. Daily he gains a few yards of ground. Beware, when the moment comes that cannot be postponed, lest you find yourselves already bound hand and foot by the insidious net that is being woven around you. Shake off its meshes here and now. Here and now form yourselves into the strongest possible union without waiting for the hesitant to join it. Swear by your honor not to leave unanswered the approaching call to arms.

Ibid.

215 a.   Whether you like it or not you men of the Spanish Army, in a period when the Army is the repository of the sole essentials and practices in which histories permanence is still integrally manifested, there is going to fall to the lot of the Army once again the task of taking the place of a non-existent state. Once the future of Spain is placed in the hands of Army, two diametrically opposed reefs must be guarded against, either of which is capable of wrecking the enterprise. These two reefs are excessive humility and excessive ambition.

1.   *Excessive humility*: It is much to be feared that the Army may allot itself the too agent, and modest role of a mere demolition and hasten to pass the Government into other hands. In this case, two equally mistaken solutions can be foreseen:

a.   A Government of notabilities, or an assembly of eminent men, chosen for their respective reputations, without regard to the political principles they profess. This would stultify possibilities of the hour. A State is more than an aggregate of so many technical abilities. It is more than a good board of directors; it is the historic instrument for the fulfilment of a people's destiny. Without a clear consciousness of its destiny, a people cannot be led. But it is just the power of interpreting that destiny and finding avenues for its accomplishment that constitutes statesmanship. A team of distinguished gentlemen who did not coincide in holding one political faith would amount to no more than a more or less good board of directors, destined to wither away for lack of any popular enthusiasm around them.

b. A coalition Government, or collection of representatives from the various parties that might lend themselves to inclusion in the Government. To the essential sterility of the previous solution, this solution would add that of amounting in practice to nothing but a relapse into party politics; in concrete terms, the politics of the Right, since it is obvious that the parties of the Left would not be willing to participate. In other words, what might have been the beginning of a promising national State would be left once more reduced to the victory of one class, one group, or one sectional interest. Such would be the perils of an excessive humility.

But the contrary is also to be feared. Let us consider it:

2. *Excessive ambition*: I do not mean—let us be clear about this— excessive personal ambition on the part of Army men, but historical ambition. This would occur if the Army leaders, realizing that a good board of directors is not enough, but that it is essential to arouse the feeling of a common task and a national interpretation of a historic moment, should seek to be the arousers of it themselves. In other words, if the Army, who had been executive agents or collaborators in the coup d'état, should set about discovering, on its own account, the doctrine and orientation of the new State. For an attempt of this kind, the Army is not possessed of enough political training. If I were trying, like so many people, to flatter the Army I should without more ado ascribe every conceivable capacity to it. By the fact that I know, what the Army does represent, the vast accumulation of silent, heroic, untarnished virtues of which it is the storehouse, I should think it an indecency to flatter; on the contrary, I deem it only loyal to serve it by an effort at clear thinking. I therefore say these things as I see them—the Army, accustomed to regard politics as not its business, possesses an inadequate angle of vision. In its championship of solutions to political problems, it suffers from a blameless simplicity. Hence through lack of doctrinal effectiveness and dialectical appeal it fails to attract popular support and youthful stalwarts. Let us not forget the case of General Primo de Rivera: filled with patriotism, courage and natural intelligence, he did not succeed in kindling a lasting enthusiasm through want of a stimulating vision of history. His "Patriotic Union," deficient in doctrinal content, stopped short at an ingenuous and well-meaning vagueness.

If Providence once again puts the destiny of our country in the hands of you Army officers, realize that it would be unpardonable to set out on the same road without a goal. Do not forget that anyone who breaks up the normal running of a State undertakes the obligation of setting up a new State, and not merely that of restoring a show of order. Remember too that the building of a new State demands ripe and resolute under-standing of history and of politics, and not a rash confidence in one's own capacity or power of improvisation.

Letter to a Spanish Officer, 1935.

PART THREE

PRACTICAL MANDATES

PART THREE: PRACTICAL MANDATES

I.

YOUTH, OUT IN THE COLD

216.   For several decades we had been listening to defeatist teachings and propaganda, and we had almost reached the stage of losing faith in ourselves. The Spain of those days was the heir of a Spain of weaknesses, of limping indecisions, of picturesque posturing: the Madrid of the Fornos cafe and the "Cuarta de Apolo," of swashbuckling journalists, of those who gaily flaunted their capes while the remains of the Spanish Empire were being lost. We had got accustomed to a life of mediocrity and coarse pretentiousness.

Parliament, 9-10-34.

217.   [T]he fact that existence should be like this in Spain, the fact that she should have no historic part to play in the life of the world, and that she should be maintaining, beneath it all, a totally unjust social system, is what makes it certain that Spain still has her revolution pending.

Ibid.

218.   [W]hen we, the men of our generation, look about us, we find a world in moral ruin; a world split by every kind of difference: and as regards what concerns us most nearly, we find a Spain in moral ruin, a Spain split by every kind of hatred and conflict.

Speech, Madrid, 29-10-33.

219.   [A] younger generation, which at this present time stands aloof from the Ministerial parties and from those of the Opposition alike, is not doing so—as you sometimes say—from an itch to play at being little gentlemen-fascists. Nothing is further from our intentions . . . it is doing so because our generation, which has perhaps thirty or forty years of life before it, will not resign itself once again to continuing to live in that flat layer bounded by lack of historic interest on the one hand and lack of social justice on the other.

Parliament, 6-6-34.

220.   All of us who made our appearance in the world after cataclysms like that of the Great War, and the Crisis, or after events like the Dictatorship and the Spanish Republic, feel that there lies hidden in Spain something that clamors more insistently every day to be brought

up to light . . . a revolution which has two veins: the vein of a profound social justice, which it is utterly essential to install, and the vein of a deep traditional feeling, springing from a tradition in the very marrow of Spanish bones, which resides, maybe, not quite where many people suppose, and which must at all costs be rejuvenated.

Ibid., 3-7-34.

221.   [I]f a generation has a duty to enter politics, it cannot do so equipped with the repertory of the half-dozen phrases that have seen many another generation through its political career.

Ibid.

222.   As always, and without mental reservation, we are thinking of Spain and of nothing else but Spain, because Spain is something more than a historical circumstance, because Spain can never be something that stands in opposition to the sum total of her lands and to each one among them.

Ibid. 4-1-34

223.   If they want to preserve the continuity of this melancholy, bedraggled, dismal Spain, which needs a desperate remedy every two years, they need not count on us. That is why we stand alone, because we see that there has got to be a new Spain created, a Spain that can escape from the double grip of hatred and fear by the only way out that is decent and noble, that is, upwards. That is why our slogan "Up with Spain!" has now become more prophetic than ever. We seek an upward way of escape for Spain, for a Spain once more capable of wholly providing her people with the three things our slogan proclaims: Patria, bread, and justice.

Speech, Madrid, 2-2-36

224.   We need two things: a nation, and social justice. We shall not have a nation so long as each one of us regards himself as the holder of a separate interest, the interest of a group or a faction. We shall not have social justice so long as each one of the several classes, in a system of conflict, seeks to impose its own domination upon the rest. Therefore, neither Liberalism nor Socialism is capable of providing us with the two things we need.

New Light in Spain, May 1934.

225.   Spain needs her revolution; Spain needs a revolution that shall give her back the sense of having something to do in the world, and establish her upon an endurable social foundation. . . . The Spanish social

foundation is soaked and riddled with injustice; a great part of the Spanish people are still living at the level of the beasts. The Spanish country, the Spanish nation, needs a complete reorganization of its economy, it needs an entirely new social sense, and it needs to feel itself united in a collective mission to be accomplished.

Parliament, 21-3-35.

226.   [U]p to now all revolutions have been incomplete, since none of them has served the national idea of the Patria and the idea of social justice at the same time. We integrate these two things: the Patria and social justice; and resolutely, categorically, upon those two unalterable principles we seek to make our revolution.

Speech, Valladolid. 4-3-34.

227.   When confronted with the resolute will to attack, a cold passive intention to resist is not enough suffice. One faith must be opposed by another. Not even in the greatest imperial times, when so much exists that is worthy of preservation, is the passive aim of preserving it sufficient. A nation is always a job to be done, and Spain is so in a very special way. Either the executrix of a world mission, or the victim of a speedy process of disintegration.

Before the Elections, "Arriba," 16-1-36.

228.   What is material can be saved by no-one; the thing that matters is that the catastrophe on the material plane shall not wreck the essential values of the spirit too. And these are what we seek to save, cost what it may. . . .

Speech, "Spain and Barbarism," Valladolid, 3-3-35.

229.   [S]omeone may ask: "Why introduce politics into the University?" For two reasons: first, because nobody, however much he may specialize, can detach himself from the common interests that all politics pursue. Secondly, because speaking candidly about politics means avoiding the sin of those who, cloaked in "non-political" hypocrisy, smuggle politics into the realm of learning.

S.E.U. Lecture, "Law and Politics," 11-11-35.

230.   [The mission of the youth of Spain is] quite clear: to carry out, itself, the building of a complete and harmonious Spain: by itself, by youth itself which feels and understands these things, without middlemen or trustees.

Youth Out in the Cold, "Arriba," 7-11-35.

231.   If the service of Spain is something eternal and not to be sub-orned, against which the conspiracies and pitfalls of the times can be of no avail, then for this highest service—in which the laying down of life itself means little—we must painstakingly draw instruction from every available source. And in order to harvest these lessons, shrewdly Spanish as they are, we ourselves are preaching the rediscovery of the authentic veins in Spain.

232.   [W]e ourselves should be but one party more if we should start enunciating a program of concrete solutions. Such programs have the advantage of never getting carried out. On the other hand, when one possesses a fixed feeling in regard to history and life, that feeling itself provides the solutions when faced with concrete facts, just as love tells us in what cases we ought to fight and in what cases we ought to embrace, though a true feeling of love has no sort of ready-made program of embraces or of strife.

Speech, Madrid, 29-10-33.

233.   Merely to embark on the loftiest of enterprises will render utterly impossible the engendering of such a state of mind as that which enabled the criminal attempt in Catalonia to take place.

234.   [Y]ou shall see how we will rebuild the dignity of man, and upon it we will rebuild the dignity of all the institutions which together compose the Patria.

Speech, Madrid, 19-5-35.

II.
THE INSTRUMENT OF THE REVOLUTION

235.   [B]y way of remedy they suggested to us, with charming ingenuousness, a pure and simple return to the ancient traditions, as if tradition were a "state" and not a "process," and as if it were easier for peoples than for men to perform the miracle of moving backwards and returning to childhood.

Between "the one and the other of these attitudes it occurred to some of us to consider whether it would not be possible to achieve a synthesis of the two things: revolution, not as an excuse for setting everything rolling, but as a surgical opportunity to reshape everything with a steady pulse, in compliance with a norm; and tradition, not as a remedy, but as a substance; not with a mind to copy what was done by the great ones of the past, but to divine what they would do in our circumstances.

Tradition and Revolution, August 1935.

236.   As the fruit of this restless reflection on the part of one or two, the Falange was born. I doubt whether any political movement has come into the world by a more austere interior process, more rigorously worked out, and with a more real sacrifice on the part of its founders, to whom—who shall ever know it as well as I do?—few things come harder than having to shout in the streets and to endure the shame of making oneself a public show.

Ibid.

237.   Our brethren of the J.O.N.S., directed by Ramiro Ledesma, were the first in opening the difficult breach. They were the first guerrilla band of the new style, they were the cocks of March, crowing inured and scandalous, singing the gracious springtime of the Spains, that which now gives us everywhere its irresistible budding of green.

Article "F.E. & J.O.N.S.," 22-2-34

238.   Our movement . . . proceeds directly out of the revolution of the 14th of April. The moment of our appearance over Spain was the 14th of April. That date, as you all know, has been looked at from very different points of view: like all historical dates, it has been regarded with a good deal of stupidity and a good deal of ignorance.

Speech, Madrid, 19-5-35.

239.   Here we have, in the earth now, one of our best comrades. He gives us the magnificent lesson of his silence. Others, comfortably, will advise us, from within their houses, to be more aggressive and tougher in reprisals. But Matías Montero did not give advice, or even speak: he contented himself with going out in the street to do his duty, well knowing that what awaited him in the street was probably death. He knew this because he had been warned in advance. Shortly before his death he said: "I know I am threatened with death, but it makes no difference to me if it is for the good of Spain and of the cause." It was not long before a bullet struck him right in his heart, the crucible of his love for Spain and for the Falange.

Comrade Matías Montero Rodriguez! Thank you for your example. May God grant you eternal rest, and deny rest to us until we are able to reap for Spain the harvest your death has sown.

Spoken at the burial of Matías Montero, 10-2-34.

240.   Another fallen comrade on the altars of Love. He knew how to fulfil a sacred mission within the *Falange Española de las J.O.N.S.*, and the Marxian lead cut short his life before crossing the threshold of the Patria reborn.

For fighting for love, hate has slain him. Comrade: your sacrifice shall not be in vain! All we who can still raise our arm in salutation over your grave, know how to follow your magnificent example. We all are ready, like you, to come to the supreme sacrifice in order to fulfil our mission. Mission in the pure sense of the word, the religious sense. Spain, which is not a territory nor a fantasy born of overheated imaginations, but a reality intangible and supreme; Spain, which is the efforts of our brothers, the glorious exploits of our fathers and the fertile blood of our forebears, is threatening to die today through cowardly neglect. And it is we, the national-syndicalists, who are called to come to her aid, to succor her, to help her rise again. Blessed be the Falange if it leads us to death for Spain! We have always before us that Spain is "one unity of destiny" in the future; let us know how to prove, face to the world and face to the sun, with Spanish pride, that if we are boys in age, we yet are men enough to die and live for Spain in the fulfilment of a holy duty.

I counsel you to close your ears to those people who, now as always, will be piteously lamenting our comrade and may perhaps advise you to go all out for reprisals. I ask you to show them by your behavior now you are able to endure all things, drawing your spirits and courage from the blood of our brothers—that blood which is again becoming the rich fertilizer of a future harvest from Spanish soil—that you may pursue your path undaunted.

Perhaps they will tell you, in insufferably patronizing tones, that you should not stay in our ranks, that you should "take a grown-up man's advice" and give up this "madness." Reply that men are not measured by bodily growth or spoken words: men are to be seen and measured in the field of deeds, of action, which is our field. And if it is true that we are mad, blessed be the madness of this love of ours which leads us to bestow on our native land the most precious thing she has given us: our blood!

Tell them roundly, and make them clearly understand, that they are the ones responsible for our comrade's death, by their selfishness, incompetence and cowardice; that this life-and-death problem that Spain is confronted with cannot be solved by words: that while they sit in their houses or in cafés "putting Spain to rights," we are out in these streets of Spain which seem destined to be continually watered with the blood of her sons, cruelly and treacherously murdered for the sole crime of possessing hearts—of possessing, above all, the hearts they lack themselves; and, finally, that we had sooner all of us die to the last man, than go on wallowing in infamy and shame.

Once more we find ourselves called to render funeral homage to a fallen comrade. Vile, cowardly, base-born is the man who would now draw back from the front rank: such a one is not worthy to be called a comrade of the dead in this supreme brotherhood of the Falange.

Once more: Falanges! Attention! All, in line of battle, in the van as always and more than ever before. There is one more now among the martyrs of Spain. José García Vara: Presente! *Arriba España*!

"Arriba," 11-4-35.

241.   We have knowingly chosen for ourselves the hardest road, and with all its difficulties, with all its sacrifices, we have been able to bring to light one of the heroic veins—for all I know, the only one—that still remained beneath the soil of Spain. A few words, a few material means, have been enough to win the post of honor, in the ranks where men die, for eighteen of our young comrades to whom life offered every promise. We, without means, with this poverty, with these difficulties, are gathering all there is of fertility and value in our Spain. And we want the difficulties to go on, to the end and after the end: we want life to be hard for us before victory and after victory. A few days ago, I reminded a small audience of a line from a Romantic poet, who wrote: "I seek not Paradise, but rest." It was a romantic poem of the return to sensuousness; it was blasphemy, but a blasphemy based on a true antithesis: it is certain that Paradise is not rest. Paradise is opposed to rest. In Paradise no-one lies down: they stand, vertically, like the angels. We, then, who have set upon the road to Paradise the lives of the best among us, seek a Paradise arduous, erect, implacable; a Paradise that never knows repose and has, standing at its gateway on either side, angels with swords.

Speech, Madrid, 19-5-35.

242.   God did not guide your hand, comrade, when you wrote: "If F.E. goes on in that literary and intellectual tone, it will not be worth risking one's life to sell it."

Well then, you yourself, who are now training your mind at the University and dreaming of a better Spain: what would you gladly risk your life for? For a libel-sheet calling Azaña an invert and the Socialist ex-ministers thieves? For a weekly paper in which we were trying to trace the lines of the future in poor, feeble, inexpressive language lacking any promise of things to come?

Maybe if we wrote like that more people might understand us at the outset. Perhaps, too, we might find it easy to stir up lucrative scandal. But then what we should have sold for the single dish of facile success would be no less than the glory of our high engagement. . . .

To make a paper like the "Heraldo" is a simple thing: one need only ensconce oneself in bad taste, stagnate in cafe circles and whet one's effrontery. But Spain has been on the point of receiving shameful burial with "Heraldos" and suchlike for her winding-sheet.

Student comrade: turn against us, on the contrary, if one day you find we have grown careless of the vigor of our style. Be vigilant lest in our pages the clarity of our mental outline should grow dull. But do not give way to the spirit of laziness and coarseness when it tempts you to pay it court.

And as for whether it is worthwhile dying for this, simply bear in mind the lesson of one of our best, Matías Montero, whom every morning we have to grieve for. Matías Montero risked his life to sell "F. E." and when he was dead and the papers he had in his pockets were gone through, there came to light an article of his, which adorned these pages, in which he did not call Azaña an invert or the Socialists thieves, but spoke of a brighter and better Spain exactly in this very style of ours.

Letter to a student who complained that "F.E." was not tough, "F.E.,"
19-4-34.

243.   Our movement . . . is not a manner of thinking, it is a manner of being. We must not set before us political construction and architecture alone. We have to adopt, in our entire life, in every one of our actions, an attitude that is human, profound, and entire. This attitude is the spirit of service and sacrifice, the ascetic and military view of life.

Speech, Madrid, 29-10-33.

244.   Here nobody is anybody, only a piece on the board, a soldier in this task which is ours and Spain's.

Speech, Valladolid, 4-3-34

245.   There are only two serious ways of life: the religious way and the military (or, if you like, there is only one, for there is no religion that is not a militia, and there is no militia that is not quickened by a religious feeling), and the hour has now come for us to realize that it is by this religious and military interpretation of life that Spain is destined to be restored.

Parliament, 6-11-34.

246.   Discipline and service play over the heads of a generation which seeks to render impossible any fresh attack upon the integral and eternal existence of Spain.

247.   The Militia hoists its recruiting-standard in every corner of the national conscience. For those who still preserve their dignity as men and

patriots. For those whose pulses still beat to the throb of Spanish blood and whose spirits still hear the voice of their forebears, buried in their ancestral soil, while their hearts ring with the familiar echo of the glories won by the men of their nation and race that cry out for perpetuation.

Heroic Sense of the Militia, "Haz," 15-7-35.

248.   The Militia is an essential, an indispensable necessity for men and peoples who seek to survive, an irresistible imperative for all who feel that their Patria and the continuity of its mission are pleading in a desperate torrent of cries, in a surging wave of imperial and imperious voices, for them to muster in one hierarchic disciplined force under the command of one leader, in obedience to one doctrine, in the practice of one single generous and heroic soldiering.

Ibid.

249.   Our youth, as if by a miracle, has discovered a vein of heroism and worth which lay as if hidden, buried deep down; and it comes out with a temper surpassing the best temper of old. There you have the list, in which figures Matías Montero, the founder of the Catholic Syndicate of Students, who even when he knew he was threatened with death did not vary his route home to his house. Jesús Hernández, a child of fifteen . . . livid, in his dying delirium, could still sing between clenched teeth the old song of the J.O.N.S.: "I seek a Spanish death."

Manuel Carrión, manager of a San Sebastian hotel. You think of him as calm, suave, peaceful, don't you? . . . a model of complaisance and tact. But one day he heard the call of the heroic, and he composed some sheets in Basque and Castilian and went out to distribute them in the streets. He was threatened with death, and one day they shot him, in the back. He died without conceding the slightest importance to life. All that interested him was the victory of the ideal for which he shed his blood. . . . Today we have thirteen comrades in prison at Seville, including one who, when Manuel Garcia died, gaily and with his face to the foe, picked him up in his arms that he might not be mutilated by the mob, and stumbling, falling, and rising again, made his way to a place of safety, and then, kissing him on the forehead, said to him: "Arriba España!" Do you not think we have found the fertility of Falange Española in deeds like those I have quoted?

Speech, Málaga, 21-7-35.

250.   The Falange is like that too. We who do battle in it have to renounce comforts, rest, even old intimacies and deep affections. We have to have our flesh ready to be torn by wounds. We have to reckon death— as enough of our best men have truly taught us—as an act of service.

Speech, Don Benito (Badajoz), 28-4-35.

251.   None of that, gentlemen; things are not going well, because we can see before us a more powerful and better organized revolution than that of last October, and because we are not willing that our sons shall feel the shame of knowing that there are men working from dawn to dusk for a plate of garlic and breadcrumbs and that many Spaniards live in pigsties.

We are not in agreement with any of that. We are not in agreement that there must be no shooting in the streets because things are going so well; if necessary, we will rush into the street ourselves and start shooting so that things shall not remain as they are.

Speech, Málaga, 21-7 35.

252.   [I]f our aims should in some event need violence to attain them, let us not stop short at violence. For who ever said, in speaking of the phrase "Anything short of violence!" that the supreme hierarchy of moral values resides in amiability? Who said that when our feelings are insulted, before we react as men, we are under the obligation to be amiable? Yes, very well, dialectic then as the first instrument of communication. But the only dialectic possible is that of fist and pistol when the offence is to Justice or to our native land.

Speech, 9-10-33.

253.   If there should be no other means than violence, what of it? Every system has been set up by violence, including even the mild Liberal one (the guillotine of '93 has far more executions to its name than Hitler and Mussolini put together). Violence is riot to be condemned categorically. It is so when employed against Justice. But even St. Thomas, in extreme cases, permitted rebellion against a tyrant. Thus, then, the use of violence against a victorious sect that sows discord, denies the national continuity, and obeys instructions from abroad—like the Amsterdam International, Freemasonry, and so on—on what grounds is the system implanted by such a use of violence to be regarded as illegitimate?

While Spain sleeps her Siesta, "Haz," 19-7-35.

254.   We will not vegetate amid the old order. Under it, Spain endured international humiliation, internal disunion, distaste for great enterprises, and the oppression, dirt, and subhuman living conditions of millions of human beings. . . . Spain has to be "mobilized" from top to bottom—put on a war footing. Spain needs to reorganize herself at one bound, not to stop in bed like an invalid without the will to be cured, resting amidst the ointments and plasters of a good administration.

Ibid.

255.   [W]e who are neither of the Right nor Left, who know that each of these attitudes is incomplete, but realize none the less that all the human material at Spain's disposal stands either on the Left or on the Right as if awaiting the voice of a redeemer. . . .

Speech, Madrid, 2-3-36.

256.   [T]he members of this youth, of which I form part, consider it not merely a bad thing that there should be a dictatorship of the Right or a dictatorship of the Left, but even bad that there should be such a thing as a political Right or Left at all.

Parliament, 19-13-33.

257.   We are neither in the Monarchist reactionary group nor in the Populist reactionary group. We, faced with the fraud of April the 14th, the swindle of April the 14th, cannot belong to any group possessing a more or less concealed reactionary or counter-revolutionary aim, because it is precisely we who accuse the 14th of April, not of having been violent, not of having been uncomfortable, but of having been barren and of having once again frustrated the long-delayed Spanish revolution. That is why the thing we are doing in the teeth of every insult and every misrepresentation is to go out on the streets and pick up, from among those who had it and threw it away and those who will not pick it up, the feeling, the Spanish revolutionary spirit which sooner or later, by peaceful means or violent, is going to give us back that community in our historic destiny and that deep social justice of which we stand in need. That is why our regime, which will have this in common with all revolutionary regimes, that it springs thus from discontentment, protest, and a bitter love of country, will be a wholly national regime, without the flag-wagging and slick speeches of decadence, but spliced onto the true, the arduous, the eternal Spain wherein lies hid the vein of the genuine Spanish tradition. It will be social at heart without demagogy because that is not needed, but implacably anti-capitalist and implacably anti-communist.

Speech, Madrid, 19-5-33.

258.   [W]e feel ourselves to be, in the most explicit sense, not the vanguard but the complete army of a new order that must be implanted in Spain; that must be implanted in Spain, I say, and because Spain is what she is, I ambitiously add: a new order that Spain is destined to communicate to Europe and to the world.

Speech, "Spain and Barbarism" Valladolid, 3-3-35.

259.   The Falange serves two extremisms and two mysticisms: that of the perpetual revolution, the Christian and civilizing one, and that of the present-day modern revolution, the irredentist and popular one. The Falange can make clean, definite and bright everything dirty, uncertain, distorted, and obscure in the Left and the Right, but both in the Left and in the Right it answers to deep roots, but ill-cultivated ones which have developed into diseased and crooked trees. From this two-fold correction springs the integrity of our State, which is bound by its two extremisms to the depths of a land that in great measure has preserved itself traditional and Catholic, and to the depths of a land that on the other hand is seething with modern popular irredentisms. In this way the Falange, in its ordered revolution, allies a consciousness of modernity with a consciousness of eternity, that is, a fully realized historical consciousness.

In Rough Weather.

260.   [N]ot for anything will our movement link its destinies to the interest of a group or class nesting beneath the superficial discrimination of Right or of Left.

Speech, Madrid, 29-10-33.

261.   [M]any people who supposed us to have come into the world in order to risk our lives in defense of their personal peace and quiet have been vilifying us, even in Conservative journals, for not handing ourselves over to be murdered; they had been imagining that we were risking our lives and those of our young comrades for the purpose of preventing any interference with their own repose.

Parliament, 3-7-34.

262.   [A]s all types and conditions were to be found in the world, and as one of the characteristic traits of the Spaniard is his complete lack of interest in understanding his neighbor, nothing could have made less impression on the Falangist's sense of the dramatic than the interpretations of him that blossomed forth all around in the minds of friend and foe alike. From those who without mincing words took us for an organization that existed for the purpose of beating people up, to those who in more intellectual fashion judged us to advocate the absorption of the individual by the state; from those who hated us as representatives of the blackest reaction, to those who thought to love us dearly in order to find in us a future safeguard for their stomachs, what rubbish have we not had to read and hear spoken concerning our Movement! All in vain we have travelled the country shouting our heads off at meetings; all in vain we have published papers; the Spaniard, staunch in his first and infallible

conclusions, denied us, even by way of charitable alms, what we should have valued far higher: a little attention.

Tradition and Revolution, August, 1935.

263.   [B]ecause Fascism contains a set of external, changeable and contingent features, which we would not for anything take over; people, who are seldom disposed to draw nice distinctions, heap upon us all the attributes of Fascism without regarding the fact that we have only taken from Fascism those essentials which are permanently valid. . . .

[T]hat sense of belief that the State has something to do and something to believe is the part of Fascism that has a permanent content, and that may well be detached from all the excrescences, incidentals and trappings of Fascism, among which there are some things that I like and others that I do not like at all.

Parliament, 3-7-34.

264.   If we have worked so hard and endured a little danger—which does not matter—in pouring out into the fields and cities of Spain to preach this Good News of ours, it is—as you have been told already by all my comrades who have spoken here before me—it is because we have no Spain now. We find Spain divided by three kinds of secessions: local separatism, party strife, and class warfare.

Speech, Valladolid, 4-3-34.

265.   The Falange does not exist. The Falange is of no importance whatever. That is what they say. But already our words are in the air and in the soil. And we, in the prison yard, smile in the sunshine. This spring sunshine in which so many buds are opening.

Article "Prieto draws near the Falange," 23-5-36.

266.   Ever since we have been declared nonexistent, not one aspect of Spanish life but is girt round with our presence. I am no longer speaking of "fascism" or "anti-fascism." I am speaking, specifically, of the ideology and vocabulary of the Falange. It is enough to recall to your minds those words that used to be employed as political labels as little as three years ago: "Right," "Left," "the party of Order," "democracy," "social reformers"—who would dare to deny their staleness now? Even movements that served a considerable purpose in their day—would they, without retouching, still evoke in your mind their ancient list of connotations: "religion," "patria," "family," "property"? Clearly, each one of these themes still ploughs its furrow in the elemental human verities; but they can no longer spring forth in the same way. The words are still

charged with interest; but the music has grown sadly antiquated. The political struggle has taken on a fresh tone and a fresh depth. Those not in the Marxist ranks have finally realized that Marxism has to be met by digging down to the very roots that it probes itself. Put simply: any antidote to Marxism is useless that does not spring from this consideration, that the world . . . is witnessing the culminating moments in the last stage of an epoch. Maybe that of the liberal-capitalist epoch: maybe that of some other, of which liberal-capitalism was the final period. We stand before the imminent menace of a "barbarian invasion"; one of those historical cataclysms that regularly operate as the colophon to every Age. Never has frivolity been less legitimate than now. Seldom has existence possessed the religious and militant quality it has today. The gashes in the life of our times refuse to scar over falsely. The last reserves of vitality must be drawn upon: those reserves which in ascendant times achieved the building up of nations. Hence the watchword of our days: "National," uttered as a summons to one mission and one task, not as a vague assumption underlying all the tasks of all the parties. Many today fly the National pennant. But in active politics, taken in this exact, poetical, militant significance, the first to advance the word "national" were ourselves, the men of the Falange Española.

And with it goes a whole system of dialectics and of poetics, a whole strict outline of form, composed more than anything else of renunciation. At the beginning we were few, and our voice was feeble. At no time have we disposed of great organs of publicity. We held rallies, but they were practically always ignored by a Press partly hostile and partly jealous. Yet through the mysterious channels by which the religious idea is disseminated, our theses steadily continued to catch on and to spread. At this moment there is not a single Spanish politician who has not more or less admittedly adopted points and angles taken from our vocabulary.

Ibid.

267.   It astounds me that after three years the immense majority of our countrymen should persist in judging us without having begun to show the faintest sign of understanding us, and indeed without having even sought, or accepted, the slightest information. If the Falange is consolidated into something permanent, I hope all will feel remorse that so much blood should have been shed because no calm attention was forthcoming to open a breach for us between the fury of one side and the apathy of the other.   Will of José Antonio.
268.   While so many inflated shams collapsed at the first blow of adversity, the Falange, poor and persecuted, has alone maintained a joyous faith in the resurrection of Spain, and a stern front against assassination and outrage.

Sheet written in the dungeons of the Security Police Headquarters,
14-3-36.

269.   We are here to fight for an authoritarian State that shall do as
much with its wealth for the humble as for the powerful.

Speech, Madrid, 29-10-33.

270.   For these things, which are not negotiations but jobs to be done,
unstinting effort. Beneath the shade of this banner we are indeed ready
to enlist, as the first or the last, in a National Front. Not to win an election
whose result is ephemeral, but with a permanent vocation. It seems
abominable to us that the fortunes of Spain should have to be staked
every two years on the hazards of the poll: that every two years we should
put on the tragic show in which by dint of shouting, bribery, inanities,
and insults everything permanent in Spain is jeopardized and the concord
between Spaniards is rent asunder. For a lengthy collective job of work,
we want a National Front. For a Sunday afternoon's elections, for the
futility of a few seats in Parliament, we do not. This electoral occasion
in our eyes represents nothing but a passing moment. When once it is
over, let us trust we shall not remain alone in the undertaking that these
lines foreshadow. But, alone or in company, while God gives us the
strength, we shall go on—without pride but without flagging—with our
hearts at peace in this our workmanlike and soldierly enterprise.

Before the Elections, 1936

271.   In vain the *Falange Española de las J.O.N.S.* has again and
again raised its voice against a political system that makes sport of the
Patria in the alternating quadrille of Right and Left. It has been vain to
reiterate that the destiny and the interest of our country are always the
same and cannot be looked at from the right or from the left, but only in
their whole integrity. Despite such predictions, the parties of the Left
have laid themselves out to slander us, representing us—well knowing
that they lied—as defenders of a capitalist system we think detestable,
while the people of the Right have preferred to rally to leaders who offered more comfortable programs, even though the comfortableness of
those programs involved the sacrifice of all youthful ardor and all deep
feeling for Spain. . . .

Falange Española de las J.O.N.S. has nothing immediate to do in this
chaos into which Spain has sunk, in this putrefaction, stinking higher and
higher to heaven, of a political system in its last throes.

Manifesto to Spain, "F.E.," 26-4-34.

272.   If the result of the election scrutiny is adverse, dangerously adverse, to the eternal destiny of Spain, the forces of the Falange will relegate the proceedings at the election scrutiny to the uttermost limbo of contempt. If, after the scrutiny, whether victorious or defeated, the enemies of Spain, the representatives of that materialistic interpretation of which Spain is the contradiction, seek once more to seize power, then once more the Falange, unblustering but unflinching, will be at its post, as it was two years ago, one year ago, yesterday, and always.

Speech, Before the Elections, Madrid, 2-2-36.

273.   Our Falange, the bearer of the new faith, will make Spain a nation again and will implant social justice in her; will give her bread and faith. Worthy fare, and imperial joy.

New Light in Spain, May 1934.

274.   May God grant that its innocent ardor may never be made use of in any other service than that of the great Spain which is the Falange's dream.

Will of José Antonio.

III.
TASK OF THE REVOLUTION

275.   The essential thing is the historical and political sense possessed by the Movement: the retention of its validity into the future. This indeed must be clear in the heads and hearts of those who are in command.

Letter to the Armed Forces of Spain, written secretly from the Model Prison, Madrid, 4-5-36

276.   We have, as Westerners, Spaniards and Christians, to begin with man, with the individual, in the building up of a new order; we have to begin with man, and continue through man's organic units. Thus, we ascend from the man to the family, and from the family to the Municipality in one way and the Syndicate in another, and we reach the culminating point of the State, which is to be the harmony of them all.

Speech, Madrid, 19-5-35.

277.   Here is what is demanded by our complete feeling of the Patria and the State which shall serve it:

That all the peoples of Spain, however diverse, shall feel themselves brought into harmony in one irrevocable unity of destiny.

And that the political parties shall disappear. No man was ever born a member of a political party; on the contrary, we are all born members of one family: we are all citizens of one Municipality; we all press forward in the exercise of one task of work. If these, then, are our natural units, if the family and the Municipality and the corporation are the realities of our lives, why should we require the intermediate and pernicious instrument of the political parties, which, in order to unite us in artificial groups, begin by disuniting us in the matter of our genuine realities? We want less Liberal word-mongering and more respect for the deep liberty of man.

We want all to feel themselves members of one solemn and entire community; in other words, the tasks to be carried out are many: for some the work of the hands; for others, that of the intellect; for others again, instruction in behavior and refinements of life. But in a community such as we strive after, let it be known henceforth, there must be no passengers and no drones.

We want no song about individual rights of the kind that can never be satisfied in the homes of the hungry, but that there should be given to every man, every member of the political community, by the mere fact of his belonging to it, the means of earning, by his own labor, a human, just and decent living.

We want the spirit of religion—the keystone of the finest arches in our history—respected and supported as it deserves, but we do not want the State on those grounds to involve itself in functions not its own, nor to share—as it has done, perhaps for interests other than those of true religion—functions which it has the duty of performing itself. We want Spain resolutely to recover the universal sense of her own culture and history.

Speech, Madrid, 29-10-33.

278.   We want the Movement begun today, and the State that it creates, to be the effective and authoritative instrument at the service of this unchallengeable unity, this permanent unity, this irrevocable unity which is called the Patria.

Ibid.

279.   [W]e want all the peoples of Spain to feel, not just the elementary patriotism by which the land draws our hearts, but the patriotism of having a mission, the transcendental patriotism of a great Spain.

Parliament, 4-1-34

280.   Here is a great and splendid job for those who really regard the Patria as a task of work: to ease its economic life of the capitalist cupping-glass, which is destined inexorably to break out in Communism: the release, through the living network of genuine producers, of the piled-up profits that parasitical capitalism absorbs, would nourish small private ownership, would really set free the individual, who is not free when he is starving, and would fill with economic substance the true organic units: the family, the township, with its communal patrimony restored, and the Syndicate, not the mere representative of those who have to hire their labor out like merchandise, but the beneficiary of the profits earned through the efforts of all who make it up.

Manifesto, Before the Elections, 16-1-36.

281.   The only way to solve the social question is by altering the economic organization from top to bottom. The economic revolution is not to consist—as is said to be our intention by some people in these parts, the sort of people who will repeat any catch-phrase without giving it five minutes examination—in the absorption of the individual by the State and in State pantheism.

It is precisely with the individual that the complete revolution, the complete reorganization of Europe, must begin, because the one who has suffered most from this dislocation, the one who has become a mere molecule, without personality, substance, content or existence, is the wretched individual, who has been the last to undergo any of the improvements in life. The whole of the new organization and the new revolution, the whole strengthening of the State and the whole economic reorganization, will be directed towards bringing the enjoyment of those improvements within the range of these huge masses that have been uprooted by liberal economics and by the Communist attempt. Is this to be called absorption of the individual by the State? What happens is that in this system the individual will have the same destiny as the State. The State will have two quite clear aims, as we have always said; one, outwards, to strengthen the Patria; the other, inwards, to make a larger number of men happier and more human and to give them more share in human life. And the day that the individual and the State, integrated in one complete harmony, restored to one complete harmony, have a single aim, a single destiny, a single lot in life, then indeed the State may be strong without being tyrannical, for it will be using its strength for its subjects good and prosperity alone.   Lecture, Madrid, 9-4-35.

282.   The workmen know national-syndicalism only through its enemies versions. They therefore believe it to be a tool of capitalism, whereas actually one of its reasons for existence is the intention of dismantling capitalism.

283.   The workmen are the blood and soil of Spain, they are part of us. Do not take them for enemies, even if they shout against us. No, my comrades, they are not enemies, all they who cast evil looks at you when you go crying our papers for sale and when you are giving out our leaflets. They are a very part of our Falange.

"Red Front," "Arriba," 16-5-35.

284.   The idler who is a guest of life without contributing anything to the common tasks is a type destined to disappear in any well-regulated community. The role of non-paying guest is on the road to extinction in the world.

"Señoritismo."

285.   [W]e will take down the economic machine of capitalist ownership which swallows all the profits, and replace it by individual ownership, family ownership, common ownership and syndical ownership.

Speech, Madrid, 19-5-35.

286.   The Spanish State could gird itself for the fulfilment of the essential functions of Power, by exercising not merely arbitration over, but in many economic aspects complete direction of, a number of bodies that descend from a grand traditional lineage: the Syndicates, for instance, which will then no longer be parasitical outbuildings as they are in the existing set-up of labor relations, but vertical integrating bodies of all who collaborate in carrying out each branch of production.

Speech, "Spain and Barbarism," Valladolid, 3-3-35.

287.   In the Fascist State—and the workmen will get to know this soon, despite all efforts—the workers syndicates are raised to the immediate dignity of organs of the State.

1st Letter to Luca de Tena, "ABC"[8]. 22-3-33.

288.   In the economic order, *Falange Española de las J.O.N.S.* tends towards total syndicalism; that is, that the surplus value of production should remain in its entirety in the hands of the organic, vertical, producers syndicate, whose own economic power would procure it the credit necessary for production, without needing to hire it—expensively—from the bankers. This economic tendency may perhaps bear more resemblance to the German than to the Italian program.

---

[8] Six months before the foundation of Falange. See Nos. 135 and 263.—Translator.

289.   The Syndicates are professional confraternities, workers brotherhoods, but at the same time they are vertical organs in the integral structure of the State. And in fulfilling his humble, personal, daily task, a man has the assurance that he is a living and indispensable organ in the body of the Patria. The State is thus relieved of a thousand duties it unnecessarily takes upon itself today. It only reserves to itself the duties of its own mission, in the eyes of the world and of history.

Lecture "State, Individual, Freedom," 28-3-35.

290.   In a future development that may seem revolutionary but is a very ancient thing, being the system of the old European Guilds, we shall reach the point where labor is not transferred like merchandise, and this bilateral labor relationship no longer obtains, but where all who take part in the task, all who comprise and complete the national economy, will be drawn up in vertical syndicates. These will not need Equity Committees or connecting pieces, because they will work organically, as, for instance, the Army works, without its having occurred to anyone to form Equity Committees of men and their officers.

Lecture, Madrid, 9-4-35.

291.   In what we are seeking to achieve, which is something much more profound, in which the worker is going to have a much greater share, in which the workers syndicate is going to have a direct share in the functioning of the State, we are not going to make social advances one at a time like somebody giving out concessions in a haggling-match, but we will reconstruct the economic system from top to bottom after a different manner and upon different foundations; and that will be the time, Señor Gil Robles, when a far fairer social order will be achieved.

Parliament, 6-11-34.

292.   Yes, go into the country. You will see more, and better, when you create your State in it.

Go into the Country.

293.   We will go into those fields and villages of Spain to turn their despair into enthusiasm. To embody them all into one undertaking. To transform into impetus what today is the righteous ferocity of wild animals herded into compounds, without a single one of the graces or the pleasures of the life of men. Our Spain is to be found among the crags and the wilds. It is there we shall find ourselves, while in the Palace of Parliament a few cliques cage up their wingless victory.

"F.E.," 7-12-33.

294.   With intelligent agrarian reform, such as that put forward by Onésimo Redondo, and with a credit reform in order to ransom farmers, small manufacturers and small traders from the gilded claws of financial usury,—with these two things there would be a task to be completed within fifty years: the winning of prosperity for the Spanish people.

Speech, Madrid, 19-5-35.

295.   [T]wo things are needful: a credit reform, in transition towards the nationalization of the credit service, and an Agrarian Reform that shall delimit the arable areas and economic units of cultivation, carry out the revolution of installing the farming people upon them, and allow to revert to forest and pasture the lands unfit for crops, which today are scratched away at by multitudes of wretches condemned to perpetual hunger.

Manifesto, Before the Elections, 1936.

296.   Spanish rural life is utterly intolerable. Agrarian Reform is something more extensive than proceeding to the carving-up and division of great estates and the grouping-together of smallholdings. Agrarian Reform is something greater, something far more ambitious and far more complete; it is an alluring and magnificent enterprise, probably capable of achievement on revolutionary occasions alone.

Parliament, 23-7-35.

297.   To us Agrarian Reform is not merely a technical and economic problem to be studied coldly in the schools; agrarian reform is the total reform of Spanish life. Spain is nearly all countryside; the fact that in the Spanish countryside intolerable conditions of life are imposed on the farming community of human beings in the Spanish environment is not merely a problem of economics: it is a whole problem of religion and morality. That is why it is monstrous to approach agrarian reform with no standard but the economic; that is why it is monstrous to set up material interest against material interest, as if the question contained nothing more than that; that is why it is monstrous for those who oppose agrarian reform to adduce nothing but titles of inheritance, as if their opponents, whose claims are based on centuries of hunger, were merely aiming at possession of a legacy and not at the whole possibility of living as human and religious beings.

This agrarian reform also falls under two headings: first, economic reform, and secondly, social reform.

Speech, Madrid, 17-11-35.

298.   Spanish Agrarian Reform must be twofold; if not, it will be no more than a partial remedy and will probably make things worse than before. In the first place, it demands an economic reorganization of the soil of Spain. The soil of Spain is not all of it inhabitable, far from it; the soil of Spain is not all of it arable. There are immense stretches of Spanish soil where to be either a tenant farmer or a small proprietor is tantamount to perpetuating a state of want from which neither father, son nor grandson will ever see themselves redeemed. There are lands of absolute poverty from which unending toil, generation after generation, can never wring more than three or four seeds for one. To keep the inhabitants of Spain bound down to these lands is to condemn them forever to a destitution that will extend to their posterity.

The first thing to be done in Spain is to mark out which are the habitable areas in national territory. These habitable areas form a part that possibly does not exceed one-fourth of that territory, and within these habitable areas the units of cultivation must be demarcated afresh. It is not a question of great estates or smallholdings; it is a question of economic units of cultivation. There are areas where the great estate is indispensable—the great estate, not the great estate-owner, he is another thing—because only large-scale cultivation can repay the great expenses necessary if the cultivation is to be efficient. . . . There are areas where smallholding is an admirable unit of cultivation; there are areas where smallholding is a disastrous one.

Parliament, 23-7-35.

299.   And thereafter, to have the courage to let non-arable lands revert to forest, the forest for which our bald lands yearn, and to pasture, that there may be a renaissance of our greatness in stockbreeding, which made us strong and robust; to let all such lands go out of cultivation, and never again to put ploughshare into their poverty. With the arable lands of Spain once delimited, then to proceed, still within the bounds of economic cultivation, to reconstruct the units of tillage. On this our National Council has put in splendid work. On general lines, three types of cultivation may be indicated, as from this point of view the northern regions and those of the east coast can to a certain degree be bracketed. There are three kinds of cultivation: large-scale cultivation of dry land, which needs industrialization and the employment of all technical processes necessary for economic production, and which must be placed under syndical control. There is small farming, including in general all irrigated land and farming of land in humid zones; these must be split up into family units, but as the fact is that in many of these areas the splitting-up process has been carried too far and has reached the stage of uneconomic minifundia, what in many cases may be a question of splitting-up will in

others be one of grouping together to form family farming units, or family farming estates, or else they will be run by a family cooperative system for the supply of equipment and the marketing of produce. Then there are other great areas, such as the olive-groves for example, whose cultivation leaves men completely unoccupied for whole months at a time. Lands of this class need complementary work, either by means of small-scale irrigation-cropping to which the workers can transfer during the seasons of involuntary unemployment, or else by the setting up of small industries ancillary to agriculture, by means of which the rural workers may earn a living during these long periods.

Once this classification of lands is made, once these economical farming units are constituted, then the time arrives to carry out the social reform of agriculture. Now ask yourselves carefully: What, from a social point of view, does the reform of agriculture imply? It implies this: the Spanish people have been going hungry for centuries; they must be taken and redeemed from sterile lands where their want is made permanent; they must be transferred to new and arable lands; they must be installed without delay, without centuries of delay as the Law of Agricultural Counter-Reform would wish, on good lands. You may ask me: Yes, but with or without compensation to the owners? That we cannot say for certain: it depends on the financial conditions obtaining at the time. But what I do say is this: while it is being settled whether we are in a financial position to pay for the land or not, the thing that cannot be demanded is that those who have gone hungry for centuries shall continue to endure the uncertainty whether there is or is not to be an agrarian reform. Those who have gone hungry for centuries must be installed first of all; after that we can see whether the land is to be paid for or not, but he who makes the reform at the capitalist's risk is juster and more humane, and he saves a greater number of souls, than he who makes it at the peasant's.

Just now, all that is no more than a part. It means the reestablishment of our people's existence on a humane material basis; but they must also be united above, they must be given a collective faith, the supremacy of spiritual things must be restored.

Speech, Madrid, 17-11-35.

300.   This will be the real return to Nature, not in the Eclogue sense, which is that of Rousseau, but in the Georgic sense, which is the deep, austere, ritual manner of understanding the earth.

Speech, "Spain and Barbarism," Valladolid, 3-3-35.

301.   Laws that are applied with equal strict-ness to all, that is what we need. The implacable extirpation of inveterate abuses: patronage, intrigue, influence. Justice, swift and sure, which if it ever inclines shall not do so in cowardice, towards the mighty, but in benevolence, towards

the erring. But this justice can only be attained by a State assured of its own justifying reasons.

Manifesto, Before the Elections, 1936.

302.   How can anybody imagine that our attitudes are going to be influenced by a definite feeling of affinity towards one country or another? Among other reasons, because assuredly there cannot be a single one of us sitting here with an open mind who has not been influenced by many such affinities; we have all of us—some more and some less, myself in the latter group—dipped into European culture; we have all felt the influence of French literature, English education, German philosophy, and the political tradition of Italy, which is at present carrying out one of the supreme experiments, a supreme experiment that no one can escape devoting serious study to, and to which, undoubtedly, no one is without some objection or other to put forward. It is, then, a Spanish interest and a Spanish attitude that I am at this moment about to defend, just as are those, assuredly, which are going to be defended by each of you.

(On Foreign Policy) Parliament, 2-10-35.

303.   We want a foreign policy that shall be determined at all times, as to peace or war, neutrality or belligerency, by the free advantage of Spain, not by servitude to any exterior Power.

Manifesto, Before the Elections, 1936.

IV.
TACTICAL WATCHWORDS

304.   It is to be hoped that there are not still left insensate fools who seek to squander a fresh historic occasion (the final one) on serving the advantage of petty interests. If there should be, the whole of your rigor and ours would fall upon them. The banner of the national interest is not flown to cover up trafficking in starvation. Millions of Spaniards are suffering from that traffic and it is of the first urgency to remedy it. For this the great task of national reconstruction must be set in motion at full speed ahead. All must be bidden, organically and in ordered fashion, to the enjoyment of what Spain produces and can produce. This will imply sacrifices by those who today enjoy too great a station in the niggardly life of Spain. But you—tempered in the religion of service and of sacrifice—and we—who have voluntarily imposed an ascetic and soldierly sense upon our lives—will teach all to bear the sacrifice with glad faces, with the glad face of him who, at the price of some renunciations in the

material order, saves the eternal store of principles which were carried to half the world, in her universal mission, by Spain.

305.   In the centuries wherein there grew to ripeness that which was to culminate in Empire, they did not say "Against the Moors!" but "*Santiago, y cierra España*!" which was a cry of effort, of attack. We, instructed in that school, are little given to shouting Down with this, or Down with the next thing. We prefer to shout "Arriba!" "Up with Spain!" Spain, one, great, and free—not half-hearted or mediocre.

Manifesto, Before the Elections, 1936.

V.
THE IDEA OF EMPIRE,
OR DOCTRINE OF THE LAST WORD

306.   In this Spain which has never been over-industrialized, which is not over-populated, which has not been through the war; Spain, in which we still retain the possibility of rebuilding a craftsmanship that still largely survives; in which we have the stout framework of a disciplined and longsuffering mass of small manufacturers and small traders; in which we have an intact array of spiritual values; in such a Spain, what are we waiting for, in order to seize our opportunity and once again to put ourselves, ambitious as it may sound, at the head of Europe? What are we waiting for?

Lecture, Madrid, 9-4-35.

307.   This integration of man and Patria—what are we waiting for, in order to bring it about? Well, we are waiting for the parties of the Left and the parties of the Right to realize that these two things are inseparable, and now you will see that it is not some trifling incident that I am blaming them for; what I am blaming them for is this inability of theirs to face the entire problem of man's integration in his Patria.

Ibid.

308.   This is just what Spain should be setting herself to do at this hour: to assume the role of harmonizing the destinies of man and of Patria: to realize that man cannot be free and is not free if he is not living as a man, and he cannot live as a man unless he is assured of a minimum living wage, and he cannot have a minimum living wage unless the economic system is established on a different footing which shall increase millions of men's chances of benefit, and the economic system cannot be so established without a strong State able to organize it, and there

cannot be a strong State able to organize it except in the service of one great unity of destiny, and this is the Patria.

Then see how everything works better, see how this titanic and tragic struggle, between man and the State that feels itself to be man's oppressor, is brought to an end. When that is won (and it can be won and it is the key to the existence of Europe, for Europe was like that when it was Europe, and like that must Europe and Spain be again), we shall know that in each one of our acts, in the most familiar of our acts, in the humblest of our daily tasks, at the same time as we are serving our modest individual destiny, we are serving the destiny of Spain, Europe and the world, the complete and harmonious destiny of Creation.

Ibid.

309.   Spain has never yet justified herself except when fulfilling a world mission, and this is the one that is hers to fulfil today: the world is living through the last death-agonies of the liberal-capitalist order, and the world can now do no more, because the liberal-capitalist order has smashed the harmony between man and his environment, between man and his Patria. . . . We have reached the end of this liberal-capitalist epoch when we no longer feel ourselves linked together by anything above us or below: we have neither a destiny nor a Patria, because each man regards the Patria from the narrow standpoint of his party, nor yet a solid basis of common life together, a strong sense of feeling bound down to the earth. . . .

Liberal capitalism must necessarily find its outlet in Communism. There is only one deep and sincere way of avoiding the advent of Communism: that is, to have the courage to dismantle Capitalism, to get it dismantled by the very people who profit by it, if in truth they do desire to stop the Communist revolution from carrying away from before their eyes the religious, spiritual and national values that Tradition contains. If they do desire it, they should give us their aid in dismantling Capitalism and setting up the new order.

This is not merely an economic task; it is a high moral task. Men must be given back their economic property, in order that substance may once again flow back into their moral units, their family, their guild, their municipality; human life must be caused once more to become close-knit and secure, as it was in other days; and for this great economic and moral task, for this mighty task, we in Spain are in the best possible circumstances. Spain is the country which has suffered least from the rigors of Capitalism; Spain—a blessing on her backwardness!—is the most backward in large-scale capitalization; Spain can be the first to be saved from the chaos which threatens the world. And observe how it is that in every age the words that create an Order issue from the mouth of a Nation. The nation which is the first to hit upon the Words of the new age is the nation that takes her place at the head of the world. Here lies our power, if we wish, to bring it about, that the head of the world shall once again be our Spain.

Speech, Before the Elections, Madrid, 2-2-36.

VI.
FINAL INVOCATION

310.   We want no more cries of fear; we want the word of command that shall launch Spain once again, with resolute step, on the universal road of historic destinies.

2-2-36.

THE LAST MANIFESTO OF JOSÉ ANTONIO

A group of Spaniards, some soldiers, others civilians, has refused to stand by and watch the complete dissolution of the Patria. They rise to-day against the treacherous, incompetent, cruel and unjust Government which is bringing it to destruction.

We have endured five months of infamy. A kind of partisan gang has become master of the Executive. Since its advent, no hour has been peaceful, no home respected, no job secure, no life safe. While a collection of creatures possessed of the devil, and incapable of action, screams in Parliament, houses are violated by the police (when not burnt down by the mobs), churches given over to looting, and decent people arbitrarily imprisoned for indefinite periods of time. The law employs two measures; one for the adherents of the Popular Front, and the other for those who are not its active supporters; the Army, Navy, and Police are undermined by agents of Moscow, sworn enemies of Spanish civilization; an indecent Press poisons the popular mind and panders to all the lowest passions, from hatred to obscenity; not a village nor a house but has been turned into an inferno of malice; separatist movements are encouraged; starvation spreads; and in order that no final touch of black may be missing from the picture, a number of Government agents in Madrid have assassinated an illustrious Spaniard who trusted to the honor and public responsibility of the officials who were escorting him. The vile barbarity of this latest exploit has no parallel in modern Europe, and admits of comparison with the blackest pages of the Russian Cheka.

Such is the spectacle of our country at the precise hour when the world situation is summoning her afresh to fulfil a mighty mission. The fundamental values of Spanish civilization, after centuries of eclipse, are recovering their ancient authority, while other peoples who put their trust in an illusory material progress are seeing their star hourly decline; before our time-honored Spain of missioner and soldier, farmer and mariner, resplendent roads lie open. It depends on us Spaniards whether we will take them. It depends on whether we are united and at peace, with our souls and bodies nerved for the communal effort of creating a great Patria. A great Patria for all, not for a group of privileged persons. A Patria great, united, free, respected, and prosperous. To fight for this, we openly break today with the enemy forces that hold our country to ransom. Our rebellion is an act of service to the cause of Spain.

If we were but seeking to substitute one party for another, one tyranny for another, we should not have enough courage—the gage of a clean soul—to launch out upon the hazard of this supreme decision. Nor would there be men amongst us clad in the glorious uniforms of the Army, the Navy, the Air Force, and the Civil Guard. Those men know that their arms may not be used in the service of any faction, but only for the continued existence of Spain, which is what is in jeopardy. Our triumph will not be that of a reactionary group, nor will it mean the people's loss of any advantage. On the contrary: our work will be a national work, which will be capable of raising the people's standard of living—truly appalling in some regions—and of making them share the pride of a great destiny recovered.

Workers, farmers, intellectuals, soldiers, sailors, guardians of our country: shake off your resignation before the spectacle of its collapse and join with us for Spain, one, great and free! May God be with us! Arriba España!

JOSÉ ANTONIO PRIMO DE RIVERA
Alicante, July 17th, 1936.

THE WILL OF JOSÉ ANTONIO

This is the last Will and Testament of me José Antonio Primo de Rivera y Sáenz de Heredia, thirty-three years of age, bachelor, barrister-at-law, native and resident of Madrid, son of Miguel and Casilda (may they rest in peace), executed and delivered in the Provincial Prison of Alicante, on the eighteenth day of November one thousand nine hundred and thirty-six.

* * *

Condemned yesterday to death, I pray God that if He does not still spare me from coming to that last trial, He may preserve in me up to the end the seemly submission with which I contemplate it, and that in judging my soul He may apply to it not the measure of my merits but that of His infinite mercy.

I am assailed by the scruple whether it may not be vanity and excessive attachment to earthly things that I should seek on this occasion to render account of some of my actions; but since, on the other hand, I have drawn to me the faith of many comrades of mine in a measure far above my own worth (all too well known to myself, to the extent of moving me to write these words in the simplest and most contrite sincerity), and since I have even stirred many of them to face enormous risks and responsibilities, it would seem inconsiderate ingratitude to depart from them all without any kind of explanation.

It is not necessary for me to repeat now what I have so often said and written about what we founders of Falange Española intended it to be. It astounds me that after three years the immense majority of our countrymen should persist in judging us without having begun to show the least sign of understanding us, and indeed without having even sought or accepted the slightest information. If the Falange is consolidated into something permanent, I hope all will feel remorse that so much blood should have been shed because no calm attention was forthcoming to open a breach for us between the fury of one side and the apathy of the other. May that blood forgive me the part I have taken in provoking its shedding, and may the comrades who preceded me in the sacrifice receive me as the last among them.

Yesterday, for the last time, I explained to the Court that was trying me what the Falange is. As on so many occasions, I adduced and went over the old texts of our familiar doctrine. Once again, I observed how very many faces, hostile at the outset, lit up, first with astonishment and then with friendliness. Upon their features, I seemed to read these words: "Had we but known it was that, we should not be here now." And certainly, they would not have been there, nor I before a popular tribunal, nor others killing each other on the fields of Spain. However, it was too late now to avoid that, and I confined myself to paying back the loyalty and valor of my beloved comrades by securing them the respectful attention of their enemies.

It was to this that I addressed myself, not to earning myself a posthumous reputation for heroism by any tinsel gallantry. I did not assume responsibility for everything, nor adapt myself to any other variant of the Romantic mold. I defended myself with the best resources I had in my profession of barrister which I have loved so much and cultivated so diligently. Perhaps there will not be wanting posthumous critics to disfigure me for not preferring the braggart's role. To me, apart from my not being the principal actor in what is occurring, it would have seemed infamous and false to surrender undefended a life which might still have been useful, and which God did not bestow on me to be burnt as a holocaust to vanity like a set-piece in a firework display. Moreover, in defending myself I should be assisting the defense of my sister Margot and my brother Miguel, who were tried together with me and threatened with severe penalties. But as the duty of self-defense enjoined upon me not only certain reticences but also certain accusations, based on suspicions of my having been deliberately isolated in the middle of a region which stayed submissive for that purpose, I declare that this suspicion is far from being proved to my mind; and that whereas it may in all sincerity have been nourished in my mind by a thirst for explanations exacerbated by solitude, it cannot and should not now be maintained in the face of death.

One other most important point remains for me to rectify. The total isolation from all communication in which I have been living since shortly after the events began has been broken only by an American journalist, who, with the authorities' permission, asked me for some statements at the beginning of October. Until I was informed five or six days ago of the charges upon my indictment, I had had no knowledge of the statements imputed to me, because neither the newspaper-men who brought them nor anyone else were accessible to me. On reading them now, I declare that among the various paragraphs purporting to be by me, and not all of equal fidelity in the interpretation of my thought, there is one that I completely repudiate: it is that which slanders my comrades in the Falange by the charge of cooperating, in the insurgent movement, with "mercenary forces brought in from abroad." I have never said any such thing, and I asserted this flatly in Court, even though the assertion might not tell in my favor. I cannot insult a military force that has rendered Spain heroic service in Africa. Neither can I cast reproaches from here on comrades concerning whom I do not know whether, they are being wisely or unwisely led, but who most assuredly are seeking to interpret in all good faith, despite the lack of communication that parts us, my watchwords and doctrine at all times. May God grant that their ingenuous ardor may never be made use of in any other service than that of the great Spain which is the Falange's dream.

Would that mine might be the last Spanish blood to be shed in civil strife! Would that the Spanish people, so rich in good qualities at heart, might now in peace be finding its Patria, Bread, and Justice.

I do not think there is anything more I need say concerning my public life. As for my approaching death, I await it without vainglory, for it is never a gay thing to die at my age, but without complaint. May God Our Lord accept it for what sacrifice it may contain, in partial reparation for all there has been of egotism and vanity in much of my life. I forgive with all my heart everyone who may have harmed or offended me, without exception, and I beg the forgiveness of all those to whom I owe reparation for any injury great or small. Which being accomplished, I proceed to order my last Will in the following.

CLAUSES

First. I desire to be interred in accordance with the rites of the Catholic Apostolic Roman Religion which I profess, in consecrated ground, beneath the protection of the Holy Cross.

Second. I name as equal heirs my four brothers and sisters, Miguel, Carmen, Pilar and Fernando Primo de Rivera y Saenz de Heredia with mutually residuary rights among themselves if any shall predecease me without issue. If issue shall have been left, the part which would have fallen to my predeceased brother or sister is to pass to such issue in equal shares to each line. This provision shall hold good even if the death of a brother or sister shall have occurred before my execution of this testament.

Third. I do not make provision for any legacy, or enjoin upon my heirs any legally enforceable obligation; but I ask them:

A)   To make use of all my goods for the comfort and wellbeing of our aunt Maria Jesus Primo de Rivera y Orbaneja, whose motherly self-sacrifice and staunch devoted affection during the twenty-six years we have been in her care is incapable of being repaid by whole treasuries full of gratitude.

B)   In memory of me, to give some of my ordinary possessions and goods to my professional companions, especially Rafael Garcerán, Andrés de la Cuerda and Manuel Sariion, who have been so loyal year after year and so efficient and patient with my far from comfortable company. To them and all the rest I return my thanks and beg them to think of me without too much annoyance.

C)   To distribute also other personal effects of mine among my best friends, whom they know well, and most particularly among those who have longest and most closely shared the joys and adversities of our Falange Española. They and the rest of our comrades occupy at this moment a position of brotherhood in my heart.

D)   To reward the oldest servants in our house, for whose loyalty I am grateful and whose pardon I beg for the inconveniences I have caused them.

Fourth. I name as executor-accountants and trustees, jointly and severally, for the space of three years, and at the maximum customary fees, my beloved lifelong friends Raimundo Fernández Cuesta y Morelo and Ramon Serrano Suner, whom I especially ask:

A)   To go through my private papers and destroy all those of a highly personal character, those containing merely literary work, and those which are mere sketches and drafts in an early stage of development, together with any works prohibited by the Church or any pernicious reading which may possibly be found among my papers.

B)   To collect the whole of my speeches, articles, circulars, prefaces to books, etc., not for the purpose of publishing them—unless they should deem it essential—but so that they may serve as sources and authorities when this period in Spanish politics, in which my comrades and I have taken part, comes to be discussed.

C)   To provide with all expedition for my replacement in the direction of the professional business that has been entrusted to me, with the aid of Garcerán, Sarrión and Matilla, and to collect some fees that are owing to me.

D)   With the greatest speed and effectiveness possible, to convey the solemn reparations herein contained to the persons and parties to whom I refer in the preamble to this Will.

For all of which I hereby return them my most hearty thanks. And in these terms I leave my Will executed in Alicante this eighteenth day of November one thousand nine hundred and thirty-six, at five o'clock in the afternoon, written on three other sheets besides this, all paginated, dated, and signed in the margin.

PROGRAM OF THE NEW SPAIN

THE 26 POINTS OF THE FALANGE

COUNTRY—UNITY—EMPIRE

1. We believe in the supreme reality of Spain. To strengthen it, elevate it, and improve it, is the urgent collective task of all Spaniards. In order to achieve this end, the interests of individuals, groups and classes will have to be remorselessly waived.
2. Spain is a destined unity in the universe. Any conspiracy against this unity is abhorrent. Any form of separatism is an unpardonable crime. The existing constitution, in so far as it encourages any disunity, commits a crime against the destiny of Spain. For this reason, we demand its immediate abrogation.
3. We have a will to empire. We affirm that the full history of Spain implies an empire. We demand for Spain a preeminent place in Europe. We will not put up with international isolation or with foreign interference. With regard to the Hispano-America countries, we will aim at unification of culture, of economic interests and of power. Spain claims a pre-eminent place in all common tasks, because of her position as the spiritual cradle of the Spanish world.
4. Our armed forces, on land, on sea and in the air, must be as efficient and numerous as may be necessary to assure Spain's complete independence at all times and that world leadership which is her due. We shall restore to the armies on land and sea, and in the air, all the dignity which they deserve and, following their ideal, we shall see to it that a military view of life shall shape Spanish existence.
5. Spain will seek again her glory and her riches by means of the sea. Spain must aspire to become a great maritime power for her defense and for her commerce. We demand for our Motherland an equally high standing for our Navy and our Air Force.

THE STATE—THE INDIVIDUAL—LIBERTY

6. Our State will be a totalitarian instrument in the service of National integrity. All Spaniards will take part in it through their family, municipal and syndical functions. No one shall take part in it through any political party. The system of political parties will be implacably abolished, with all that flows from them—inorganic suffrage, representation by conflicting parties, and parliament of the familiar type.

7. Human dignity, the integrity of man and his liberty, are eternal and untouchable values. But only he is really free who forms part of a strong and free nation. No one will be allowed to use his liberty against the unity, strength, and liberty of the country. A rigorous discipline will prevent any attempt to poison, disunite or influence Spaniards against the destiny of the Motherland.

8. The National-Syndicalist State will permit every private initiative which is compatible with the collective interest of all and will even protect and encourage beneficial enterprises.

ECONOMY—WORK—CLASS—WARFARE

9. In the economic sphere we imagine Spain as one gigantic syndicate of producers. We shall organize Spanish society in a corporative manner by means of a system of vertical syndicates with branches of production in the service of national economic integrity.

10. We repudiate any capitalist system which ignores popular necessities, dehumanizes private property, and huddles workers into shapeless masses ripe for misery and despair. Our spiritual and national sense also repudiates Marxism. We shall organize the impulses of the working-classes, led astray today by Marxism, by exacting their direct participation in the great task of the national State.

11. The National-Syndicalist State will not cruelly ignore economic conflicts, and therefore will not stand unmoved in face of a domination of the weakest class by the strongest. Our regime will make class-war radically impossible, in as much as all those who cooperate in production will be part of an organic whole. We abhor, and will prevent at all costs, the abuse of one partial interest by another and anarchy in the field of work.

12. The first object of wealth—and our State will affirm this—is to better the people's conditions of life. It is intolerable that great masses of people should live miserably while the few enjoy every luxury.

13. The State will recognize private property as a lawful means of fulfilling individual, family and social ends, and will protect it against the abuses of the great financiers, speculators and moneylenders.
14. We uphold the tendency towards nationalization of the Banking services and also, through the medium of Corporations, that of the big public services.
15. Every Spaniard has a right to work. Public bodies will, as a matter of course, assist those who are unable to find work. Until we have built up the new structure, we will maintain and intensify all the advantages which have been afforded to the worker by the existing social laws.
16. Every Spaniard who is physically fit has the duty of working. The National-Syndicalist State will not extend the slightest consideration to those who do not engage in any definite employment and aspire to live like invited guests at the cost of the effort of others.

THE LAND

17. At all costs, the standard of life in the country must be raised. It is the permanent spring of the life of Spain. To this end, we bind ourselves to carry out without hesitation the economic and social reform of Agriculture.
18. We shall enrich agricultural production (economic reform) by the following means:
    a. By assuring for all products of the soil a remunerative minimum price.
    b. We shall insist that a great part of what is today absorbed by the towns in payment of their intellectual and commercial services shall be returned to the land so that it may be sufficiently endowed.
    c. By organizing a real National Agricultural credit scheme which, by advancing money at low interest to the laborer on the security of his goods and harvests, will save him from usury and the domination of political bosses.
    d. By spreading the teaching of agriculture and cattle breeding.
    e. By arranging the allotment of land according to its conditions and with regard to the possible disposal of its products.
    f. By arranging tariffs so that they shall protect agriculture and the cattle industry.
    g. By the acceleration of irrigation works.

   h. By rationalizing the units of agriculture in order to suppress both the large neglected estates as well as small properties which are non-economic because of their poor return.
19. We shall organize Agriculture socially by the following means:
   a. By redistributing cultivable land in order to set up family properties and energetically stimulate the syndication of laborers.
   b. By ending the misery of the human masses who to-day wear themselves out in ploughing sterile land, and who will be transferred to new cultivable land.
20. We shall embark on an untiring campaign to increase the importance of raising cattle and reforestation, taking severe measures against any persons who may place obstacles in the way, going so far as the temporary compulsory mobilization of the whole of Spanish youth for this historic task of reconstruction of the National wealth.
21. The State will be empowered to expropriate without compensation any property which has been illegitimately acquired or enjoyed.
22. The reconstruction of the communal land of the villages will be one of the first objects of the National-Syndicalist State.
23. It is the essential task of the State, by means of a rigorous discipline in education, to build up a strong and united National spirit and to instill into the souls of the future generations happiness and pride of country. Every man will receive a pre-military education in order to prepare him for the honor of being incorporated in the National and Popular Army of Spain.
24. Culture will be organized in such a form that no talent shall run to seed for want of economic means. All those who deserve it will have easy access to the University.
25. Our movement will incorporate the Catholic spirit—of glorious tradition and predominant in Spain—in the national reconstruction. The Church and the State will arrange a Concordat defining their respective spheres. But the State will not permit any interference or activity which might lower its dignity or the National integrity.

NATIONAL REVOLUTION

26. The Spanish Traditional Phalanx of the J.O.N.S. desires a new order of things, which has been set out in the principles announced above. Its methods are preferably direct, ardent, and combative. Life is a battle and must be lived with a spirit alight with service and sacrifice.

ENJOYED THIS BOOK?

TO READ MORE, VISIT US AT

ANTELOPEHILLPUBLISHING.COM